'At last – an honest book a[bout the condi]tion of wandering pilgrim[s who don't] know where they're going, casting themselves adrift on the sea, like Columba in his rudderless coracle. Prayer for them was an exercise in giving up specific expectations, while gaining a heightened awareness in their abandonment to risk. It led Columba to the island of Iona, a magical place that forms the heart of this book. Margaret Somerville considers prayer as an invitation to an uncharted wilderness, drawing on wonderful sources from various faith traditions.'
~ **Belden Lane**, author of *The Great Conversation: Nature and the Care of the Soul*; and *Backpacking with the Saints: Wilderness Hiking as Spiritual Practice*

'Margaret's work is inspiring and necessary. This book is a trustworthy guide and a revolution of redefinition that empowers people to a path of deeper authenticity and wholeness with prayer, with self, with existence.'
~ **Chelan Harkin**, author of *The Prophetess, The Return of The Prophet from the Voice of The Divine Feminine*

'*When Prayer Doesn't Work* is not just a book – it's a wake-up call. At a time when our prayers for peace seem to echo unanswered, Margaret Somerville rethinks, reframes, and reimagines prayer as more than supplication. She invites us to shift from an I-Thou relationship with the Divine to an intimate oneness with Source, where each thought is sacred, each word is a prayer, and every action serves the wholeness of all that is. This book liberates us from the limitations of transactional prayer and reveals the profound truth that presence itself is prayer. It is a must-read for anyone seeking to embody a prayerful life, where connection replaces petition and wholeness dissolves separation. A deeply moving, paradigm-shifting guide for our times.'
~ **Arun Wakhlu**, Executive Director, Foundation for Peace and Compassionate Leadership; Member of the Board, Charter for Compassion

---

'What is prayer? Can it happen anywhere, anytime? What are we even doing when we pray? Author Margaret Somerville invites us to consider these questions, along with the possibilities that open up when we recognize that prayers can fit anywhere, and challenges the notion that there's a 'right' way to pray. *When Prayer Doesn't Work* is a grounding and accessible book for everyone who seeks connection to the divine. Here is an essential companion on the journey created by allowing the holy to rise from the ordinary; a reimagining of what it means to pray.'

~ **Heidi Barr**, author of *Collisions of Earth and Sky*, *12 Tiny Things*, and *Church of Shadow and Light*

'In *When Prayer Doesn't Work*, Margaret Somerville shares her own experiences of despair and joy, weaving them into a deeply personal narrative. As the Wise Woman, the Spinster, she becomes a guide – inviting us to reflect on our everyday lives as sacred texts, to sense the Divine in the ordinary, and to rethink, reframe, and reimagine how we approach prayer and contemplation.

'Margaret encourages us to broaden our spiritual vision, to embrace diverse perspectives, and to explore new ways of connecting with the sacred. She challenges conventional notions of prayer, especially at life's pivotal "threshold" moments:

> *Traditional prayers at threshold moments might ask for forgiveness for what has been, and for guidance for what is to be. But here's the tricky part: there is no reality other than the threshold itself. The prayer is standing in that moment of threshold. And being aware of the divine in the doorway with you. Loving you no matter what lies behind. Loving you no matter what lies ahead.*

'In the end, despite the wisdom offered by countless spiritual traditions and Holy Scriptures, we must confront ourselves – take responsibility for our actions, thoughts, and intentions – and, as Margaret puts it, "stand in that moment of threshold," facing our personal Web of Wyrd.

This book opens new pathways and windows into spiritual understanding. I highly recommend it to anyone seeking fresh inspiration in their spiritual practice. It is especially valuable for those involved in interfaith work, offering insight into a range of religious and spiritual traditions – some of which were new to me. As a Wiccan Priestess, I was particularly pleased to see respectful inclusion of paganism and nature-based religions. Thank you!

~ **Morgana Sythove**, Wiccan Priestess. International Coordinator for PFI/Pagan Federation International, The Netherlands.

'This beautifully crafted book is a precious gem sparkling with insights and practices; it awakens our heart and mind to the "Glow of Presence" in the course of our daily life.'
~ **Imam Jamal Rahman**, author of *Spiritual Gems of Islam*

When Prayer Doesn't Work is a wonderful invitation to practice being lost, to reframe and reimagine our vision in expansive ways that reach across myriad faith traditions to create a tapestry of care in a world that desperately needs it. This is the kind of book I would take with me along with Chodron's *When Things Fall Apart*. Lovely, poignant, and powerful.
~ **Patty Krawec, Wabanan Anangokwe**, author of *Becoming Kin: An Indigenous Call to Unforgetting the Past and Reimagining Our Future* and *Bad Indians Book Club: Reading at the Edge of a Thousand Worlds*

In this beautiful and timely read, Margaret Somerville highlights how, despite our theological differences, the human yearning to connect with the Divine is something we all share. As someone from the Muslim tradition, I deeply appreciated her reflections on the physicality of prayer and the importance of creating safe spaces for it to be integrated into our daily lives, including the workplace. Margaret eloquently conveys how prayer is a sincere longing for peace, presence, and purpose. This book is a powerful reminder that prayer is a universal language – one through which we all seek communion with our Creator.
~ **Kashmir Maryam**, author of *The Muslim Woman's Islamic Book Collection*, including *The Muslim's Woman's Manifest*, *Nafsi*, and *Be Soft, Be Strong: Inspirational Reminders for Muslim Women*

A deeply inspirational and personal book. Moving from being lost to reimagining ways to pray. From seeing prayer as a petition that needs to be answered to one as being connected and in the presence of the Divine instead. From one's own tradition to learning from others. It gives me hope that peace is possible both within and in our troubled world.
~ **Rev. Dr. Urzula Glienecke**, Latvian theologian, artist and activist, member of the Iona Community, Interfaith Chaplain at the University of Edinburgh

For Nan and Ernest
I traced the rainbow through the rain

When Prayer Doesn't Work

Reimagining our understanding and expectations of prayer

Margaret Somerville

wild goose
publications

www.ionabooks.com

Copyright © 2025 Margaret Somerville

First published 2025 by
Wild Goose Publications
Suite 9, Fairfield
1048 Govan Road, Glasgow G51 4XS, Scotland
A division of Iona Community Trading CIC
Limited Company Reg. No. SC156678
www.ionabooks.com

ISBN 978-1-80432-390-8
Cover image, from a painting by Sondra Rosenberg © Margaret Somerville

The publishers gratefully acknowledge the support of the
Drummond Trust, 3 Pitt Terrace, Stirling FK8 2EY in producing this book.

All rights reserved. No part of this publication may be reproduced in any form or by any means, including photocopying, electronic publishing or any information storage or retrieval system, without written permission from the publisher via PLSclear.com.

Margaret Somerville has asserted her right in accordance with the Copyright, Designs and Patents Act, 1988, to be identified as the author of this work.

Overseas distribution
Australia: Willow Connection Pty Ltd, 1/13 Kell Mather Drive,
Lennox Head NSW 2478
New Zealand: Pleroma, Higginson Street, Otane 4170,
Central Hawkes Bay

Printed in the UK by Page Bros (Norwich) Ltd

Contents

Foreword 11

Introduction 13
    What Is Prayer? 14
    How to Pray 101 15
    Who Knows How to Pray 16
    Prayer as Presence in Pain 16
    Setting Prayer up to Fail 17

Part I: Practice Sacred Space 21
  Chapter 1: Ritual and Rest 22
    The Pattern of Prayer 22
    Sabbath 25
    Tending the Fire 27
  Chapter 2: Creating Sacred Space 31
    Ordinary Rituals That Create Sacred Space 31
    Sitting in Sacred Space 32
    The Posture of Prayer 33
    Expanding the Posture of Prayer 36
  Chapter 3: Becoming a Vessel 43
    Emptied Space 43
    Clay Pots 45
    The Dancer as Vessel 48
    What Spills Out 49
    Immanent Light 51
  Chapter 4. Knowing Your Limits 55
    False Summits 55
    Finding God in the Gap 56
    Finding Something in Nothing 58
    God as a Verb in the Space Between 59
    Keeping Our Productivity in Check 59

Part II: Practice Release 65
  Chapter 5: Ground Level 66
    Teaching at Ground Level 66

      Prayer at Ground Level   67
      When Circumstances Don't Allow   69
   Chapter 6: Contemplation in Community   74
      Contemplation Does Not Have to Be Done Alone   74
      Building a Community of Hope   76
      When Prayer Becomes an Act of Service   77
   Chapter 7: Letting Go of Labels   81
      Shaped by Language   81
      Missing the Meaning   84
      Interconnected and Interdependent   85
   Chapter 8: What We Let Go and What We Carry Forward   93
      Threshold Moments   93
      Liminal Spaces Looking Back and Forward   95
      Prayer as a Liminal Space   97

Part III: Practice Naming   101
   Chapter 9: Exchanging Our Exhale   102
      Breath prayers   102
      Tonglen: the Buddhist Practice of the Exhale   104
      Anáil na Beatha: The Breath of Life   106
   Chapter 10: Naming God   113
      Being Named   113
      Hineni   114
      Breathing the Name of God   117
   Chapter 11: The Journey of Identity   121
      Gender Identity   121
      Seeing God Face to Face   124
   Chapter 12: Claiming and Reclaiming   130
      Turning to Our Pagan Roots   130
      Saving Solstice   132
      Embracing Darkness   133
      Awaiting Light   136
      The Turning   137

Part IV: Practice Wilderness   141
   Chapter 13: Getting Lost   142
      Following the Directions   142

Lost in Prayer　144
　　Chapter 14: Finding Direction　150
　　　Messengers　150
　　　At the Distance of a Bowshot　152
　　　Sitting with Wisdom　156
　　Chapter 15: Taking a New Path　162
　　　Chrysalis Soup　162
　　　Companions on the Journey　164
　　　The Wild Geese　166

Part V: Practice Nourishment　**171**
　　Chapter 16: Sharing Sustenance　172
　　　Putting the Kettle On　172
　　　Filling Our Cups　173
　　　Drinking Water　174
　　　Baking Bread　177
　　　The Bread of Life　179
　　　Breaking Bread　180
　　Chapter 17: Embracing Creativity　184
　　　The Scent of Creation　184
　　　The Shape of Creation　185
　　　The Sound of Creation　186
　　　Creating Movement　189
　　　Painting the Cave　190

Part VI: Practice Peace　**195**
　　Chapter 18: Peace Through Connection　196
　　　What Is the Point of Prayer?　196
　　　Cultivating Connection　197
　　　Prayers for World Peace　199

Epilogue　**201**

Notes　**204**

Foreword

I love books on prayer that turn our thoughts and imaginations upside down, that cause us to question our assumptions of ourselves, the Sacred, and the world around us. Margaret is a teacher, facilitator and guide, and leads with powerful humility in the pages of this book.

We need each other to explore what prayer means. I think that's what prayer is all about – recognizing the power of our naming things, of our vulnerability, of taking a chance on hope, while also holding the humility of a child, of a human being in the midst of it all. The stories in these pages remind us that while prayer is incredibly vulnerable and personal, it's also communal.

And it's especially important in the world we are living in today to embrace prayer as inter, meaning between: between layers, between meanings, between faiths. Margaret, who is steeped in the beauty of interfaith relationship, guides us into prayer from this perspective, and it is incredibly valuable for us to gently and compassionately explore how our inner world is shaped by the expansiveness of the relationships we carry and tend to.

And while we are exploring our relationship with one another, the stories in this book also tenderly remind us of who we are. We may be a speck in the infinite universe, but we are a beloved one nonetheless.

This book isn't just about reframing the way we understand prayer, but shares powerful ways to help us embody it, leaning gently into rituals and practices that help us live prayer in our bodies and lives.

As I read *When Prayer Doesn't Work*, I found myself swaying, a reminder of something I do when I need to be comforted, something I might do when I'm trying to realign myself with prayer, with God, with my own body and being. That's what this book does – brings us back, gently, to ourselves, allowing us to ask expansive questions of who we are in this world.

I want to point you to something that Margaret writes in this book:

> *'When we are not expansive in our presentation and practice of prayer, we set prayer up to fail. And we set pray-ers up for a loss of faith.*

And disconnection. But when we expand our understanding of prayer, and incorporate new practices, we create connection, which surely is the core intention of prayer. Connection to the divine. To a sense of peace within ourselves. To an awareness of the beauty that lies within us, beside us and beyond us.'

That is what I feel when I read this book, when I take in the stories that are shared within these pages: connection, awareness, intention, lack of judgement.

Just as we are trying to reframe God as someone 'up there' to someone here and present with us, in this book we have the freedom to reframe the way we understand prayer, not as something we do but perhaps as something we are. As humans, we live and breathe prayer, whether intentionally through ceremony, ritual and in community, or in those guttural, inaudible ways that spill from us when we just need to be held by the Sacred. Prayer is who we are.

This book will move you toward yourself, toward God, and back out into the world again, where prayer becomes presence. Lean in, friends. You're in good company here.

Kaitlin B Curtice, *award-winning author of* **Native *and* Living Resistance**

Introduction

I'm not sure I'll ever find the marble quarry.
The elusive spot on the south side of the Isle of Iona
may be a destination that remains forever unfound for me.
And maybe that's just as it should be.

It was my first time traveling alone to Iona,
the land that grounds my connection to now and then,
to body and breath
to heaven and earth
to humanity and the spirit world
That liminal space of thinness where I am at home
and utterly lost at the same time.
And lost I was.

The directions seemed so clear. Up the road to the back bays, first left at the crossroads and over the moors to the south-side cliffs of the island. There, the treasure trove of decades past where the distinctive green and white marble was harvested for the abbey and sacred objects of countless pilgrims. One year my antiquity- and rock-loving son snuck off to the quarry by himself and came back with pockets full of remnants and a story of scaling a thirty-foot cliff. He hung on to the marble with his clawed fingertips, the sea far beneath his precarious grasp and a spider far too close to his face. The terrifying part for him – the spider. For me – the thought that I would never have found him had he fallen.

On this summer day, after what must have been fifty trips to Iona, first with my parents, then with my own children, I was there alone for the first time. Determined to get to the quarry by myself. Instead of the destination, however, I found the journey. Following the path made by the footsteps of others seemed easy at first, until the bog was so thick that I was skipping from foot to foot so I wouldn't sink in with a slower step. My toes were squelching in my sodden socks. My body was bracing against the wind coming off the sea. My already challenged sense of direction was completely gone. After multiple attempts to reorient and redirect, I decided to practice being lost. The words that came: when there is no option but to keep going, keep going.

I recognized this as my mantra, my breath prayer, during the couple of hours that it took me to untangle myself and find the road again. But on later reflection I realized that being lost was the practice of prayer itself.

How stuck I was, growing up, in my understanding of what prayer was. So limited to words and formulae and beliefs and one inherited tradition. I failed to notice that all along my parents had been teaching me about prayer in ways that I never understood.

In a world which has lost its compass, failing to recognize the sanctity of humanity and creation at every turn, it is critical that we open our hearts and ground our feet to practices of prayer that embrace the holiness of every moment that we encounter. That embrace the traditions of those who live and work and breathe around us. That honor and uphold the voices of all who cry out in pain, isolation, grief and invisibility. That allow us to fall in love with ourselves.

How do we begin? By rethinking and reframing and reimagining.

What is Prayer?

Prepared or unprepared. If one were to break down prayer into two basic categories, there would be prayers-of-the-carefully-crafted-words and prayers-of-the-flowing-thoughts. The first type includes those handed down through generations of faithful supplicants, sometimes in languages not truly known to those using them. And also prayers composed like poetry to be delivered during a service or at a special occasion. The second type of prayer seems to come from a wellspring unfathomed, ready to slip from the lips of someone asked to pray on the spot. Each kind is a very different gift. One requires memorization from early days of religious training or from the time of composition. The other takes some level of practice or surety that the words will be there when needed. But what if we don't know how to pray? What if we haven't memorized or learned the special formulae to write prayers, or what if we do not possess the ability to draw on powers of extemporaneous prayer? Then it is time to expand our understanding of what it means to pray, how to pray, and why it is important to us.

How to Pray 101

I attended a workshop meant for people who were not faith leaders, to address their concerns about learning to pray. Each week of this month-long series featured a different faith leader giving their own take on the process of preparing prayers for a religious service. The intention was to build a bank of congregation members who felt confident enough to help lead worship services or make a hospital visit where they might be asked to pray. The focus was on the composed form of prayer, not on knowing how to recite the Amidah or Dhuhr or Lord's Prayer[1]. Different types of prayers were explained, and templates given, as well as the opportunity to practice writing prayers and offering them to the group – your basic How to Pray 101 workshop. It was surprising to see how concerned participants were about getting the words just right. Perhaps the prayers would not work if they did not write them correctly. What if I don't know how to pray?

The workshop was more anxiety-producing than nourishing, in my opinion. Participants felt compelled to name the type of prayers they were crafting. Adoration, confession, illumination, thanksgiving, intercession. Each with its specific purpose. Labeled, structured, choreographed. I was in a breakout room with a partner in which we were to compose a prayer of intercession and then deliver it back to the whole group. My prayer-writing partner was eager to find the right words and to figure out how many sentences we should have. Co-opting the plan, I asked her to talk about what was sitting on her heart. What names she needed to use to call out to the divine. We didn't finish the assignment before being called back to the main Zoom room. We had failed to produce. But the prayer we shared in a moment of connection was more authentic for me.

Who Knows How to Pray?

When I was first in seminary and ordained as a minister, I had a dear friend who began asking me to pray for different situations. A daughter getting a divorce. A mother with cancer. A best friend suffering from anxiety. And her own insecurity about her belief in God. Although her faith was wavering amidst the onslaught of circumstances where she felt as if God was not present, she did still believe that prayers were necessary. And that they would be more effective coming from me – I had a closer connection now, seeing as I was official. My prayers had a more direct line, as she saw it. So I dutifully accepted her prayer requests, and occasionally prompted her to lift her own prayers as well. But I had to tread lightly. Her belief in the power of prayer, its necessity and effectiveness, was even more deep-seated than her belief in the power to which I was praying. The danger here, of course, was when my prayers didn't work. The daughter divorced; the mother died; the prayers had failed.

The workshop that she needed was the one to address our understanding and our expectations of prayer. The one that teaches us that there are a million more categories of prayer than the composed and the spontaneous. Than the ones passed down through generations and the ones thought up on the spot. These have their place and purpose, most certainly, but what if we took the need for place and purpose out of the equation? What if we even took the need for words off the table? And opened up to people the fact that, a million times a day, we engage in prayer without actually knowing that we are praying.

Prayer as Presence in Pain

Trappist monk Thomas Merton beautifully explained that prayer is about seeking the experience of presence.[2] Yes, there are petitions on behalf of devastating conditions. There are prayers in the deepest, darkest moments of our own grief, isolation and despair. There are times when we cannot hold the anxieties that put a vice around our chest and squeeze. But if only we could know that to pray is to seek the experience of presence, with a God that is in those heaviest of moments with us – then perhaps we would be free to burst into prayer with sighs and tears and even exclamations of joy, assured that we don't need to know how to pray. Just opening up our heart and letting it feel, that is praying. Praying can be closer to an emotion than an action. And it doesn't need words, and it doesn't need training, or composition, or memorization, or formulae. It needs only the recognition that in feeling whatever you are feeling, there is more than you feeling it. And holding it.

Setting Prayer Up to Fail

When we are not expansive in our presentation and practice of prayer, we set prayer up to fail. And we set pray-ers up for a loss of faith. And disconnection. But when we expand our understanding of prayer, and incorporate new practices, we create connection, which surely is the core intention of prayer.

Connection to the divine.
To a sense of peace within ourselves.
To an awareness of the beauty that lies within us, beside us
and beyond us.

There are times when the expectations of prayer that have been trained into us lead to a loss of faith instead of a strengthening of it. A sense of abandonment and isolation naturally ensues when we are taught that prayer is a petition, or conversation with God, and we do not feel as if we hear God's response.

We wonder:
Why aren't my prayers answered?
Where is God?

These feelings may come from traditional expectations of prayer and from not thinking through what prayer might mean in our lives.

So together let us
RETHINK what we are expecting from prayer.
REFRAME our understanding of what constitutes prayer.

REIMAGINE the ways in which we are in communication
with the divine and find that experience of presence.

In exploring this we can step away from the type of prayer that is limited and limiting, that causes us to think that prayer doesn't work, and that prevents us from embracing prayer practices from other traditions and incorporating them into our own practices. Let us step away from the really difficult notion brought to interfaith work by Pope John Paul II that we can't come and pray together, but we can come together and pray. We can do both, if we open ourselves to an authentic understanding of what prayer is in our lives.

In the following chapters we will explore prayer as practices that already exist in our lives. Practices that create connection and nurture love and peace. Love for oneself, for the other, and for the mysteries of creation all around us. Love that builds a foundation of peace within our own hearts and in the numerous relationships with people we know and have not yet encountered. With a fresh understanding of prayer as a grounding force in our lives, and with the embrace of prayers from a multitude of traditions into our own practice, we will replenish a world where love and peace create justice for all beings and for our beloved home of Earth.

Let us practice being lost and finding home. Let us practice the journey without the need of finding the destination. Let us break open our hearts to embrace a new understanding.

Let us pray.

Practice

RETHINK

Let us shift our expectation from one of petition and response to one of connection and presence.

REFRAME

Let us reframe our understanding of prayer. Beyond formulaic structures or inherited words, we will explore practices that we might already engage in which create a sense of connection and presence, love and peace.

REIMAGINE

Informed by different traditions, let us reimagine how an expanded understanding of prayer practices in our communities and in our own daily practice can build bridges of understanding so that, grounded and growing, we might have the strength to work for justice in the world around us.

Part One

Practice Sacred Space

Chapter 1
Ritual and Rest

Practice
Not time set aside for prayer
But prayer in time set aside

The Pattern of Prayer

The rhythm of his breathing sounded distressed to me. An audible sucking in of air through pursed lips gave way to an even longer and more pronounced exhalation. Like a runner at the end of one mile too many, he was starved for enough air coming in through his nose, but ready to let go of more than came in. He sat on the end of his bed, his head weighted down, putting on one sock, then the other, and breathing, heavily. We knew not to disturb these moments on a Sunday morning before my father left for church, his sermon swirling through his head. Surely it was only in my imagination that I could see the cloud of words that came out with each breath and surrounded him like a blanket, thick and heavy, but also so filled with light that – yes – it must just have been the dust in the air, illuminated by the sun streaming in the window. I made myself very small and kneeled outside the door of the bedroom, just at the top of the stairs, so I could listen to him breathing. Even if I had dared to tell him his toast was ready, I don't think I would have penetrated his almost visible cloud of breath words.

I revisit those Sunday morning stealthy observations often in my wonderings. As a young child, on some level I was just worried. Was it healthy for him to be breathing in such a profound way? Had it not been the 1970s, I probably would have googled the health issues associated with such labored breaths. I was also perplexed. Was he nervous? This powerful preacher, known for his provocative sermons that challenged a wealthy and conservative congregation? Did he have to talk himself into the courage it took to proclaim the truth he saw in God's word? For an introvert by nature, perhaps these breaths were inflating the persona that we all saw as bold and confident and outspoken.

But now, two lifetimes later, I have a much clearer understanding of what I was witnessing. My father was in prayer. And I was, I am now sure, sitting in awe of the presence of the divine. I knew the moment was sacred. I didn't recognize it or understand it, but I did know not to disturb it. I was drawn to it, but didn't want to get too close. It scared me and worried me and bewildered me, but I knew there was something that happened in those moments that enabled my father to be who he was and to do what he did. He was known for his beautifully crafted, even lyrical, prayers in worship. But what I have come to understand is that his most powerful prayers were the ones he lived. Behind the Sunday morning pulpit pounder was a man deeply connected to his contemplative practices, ones that I have only recently come to realize were his forms of prayer.

Prayer always perplexed me. I grew up in a world where people were praised for having gifts in two very different kinds of praying: the carefully composed prayer or the free-flowing spontaneous prayer. My father knelt at the communion table at the very, very back of the chancel of the church, his black robe liquefying into the gray marble floor in a scene that might have called to mind the melting of the Wicked Witch of the West. You would have to be positioned just right even to catch a glimpse of him, now humbled from his powerful stance in the pulpit. But his voice, lowered to a deeper timbre, still filled every corner of the beautifully carved gothic nave of the sanctuary. The melody of his Glaswegian accent alone could have put someone into a hypnotic state, but his words, pure poetry, were the type of prayer that seeped into you like honey coating a sore throat. Perhaps it was then that I fell in love with language. With image-rich phrases and an artful combination of consonants and vowels, he created prayers that were lyrics for the song of his voice. They magnified the sense of presence of the divine, so that it even reverberated from the walls. He must have prepared these prayers after writing his sermon, for they echoed the call to action. He must have sat down to compose them after his countless pastoral visits of the week, for they held each person cradled in care, unnamed but known. But most likely they were emerging during all of the moments I now know formed his contemplative practices during the week. The parts of our family life that I cherish in memory I now see were all part of my father's response to the apostle Paul's call to pray without ceasing.

And then there is the other type of pray-er. The one who is admired for their ability to pray on the spot with words that just come to them. I must admit that when I know someone is ad libbing a prayer, I cannot focus on it. I cannot come into a meditative or reflective mindset. I'm too busy thinking about what they are going to say next, bewildered by their surety that the words will simply be there in the form they will need. As a minister myself, I lived in terror of the times when people would say, hey you, you can do that thing, praying on the spot. Can you lead us in prayer? More power to those who pray in public this way, and for all of the traditions which uphold this type of prayer as central to their practice. It is not mine. And it has taken me years to get over the feeling of failure associated with not being able to pray in this way. But it has taken me even more years to become aware that I pray in a myriad of other ways I never even realized were prayer. As I have come to recognize how many different ways my father prayed, the ones his congregation never heard, I now know that I do, in fact, pray without ceasing.

So I come to this writing with the basic premise that many of us are not fully aware of what prayer is. Or what it is for. Or if it works. Or if it is a necessary part of a life of faith. And that tied closely to this exploration is the question of what the divine is. Are we praying to or in communication with something that has been defined in a way that is wholly unsuitable for us? Raised with the constant encouragement to question and not just accept any understanding I had of my faith, little did I know that in attending seminary, the door would be opened even further to explore and reframe my relationship with my faith. Credentialed and ordained, I was finally free to be the heretic that my close colleague suggested I wait to become until after proclaiming Jesus Christ to be my Lord and Savior at my examination. Identifying with the label agnostic felt even more intimidating than coming out as queer to people who knew me and the life I had lived into my fifties. But confident now that I do not need to understand fully what the divine is in order to recognize divine presence in my life, I am open to embracing prayer that is comfortable and prayer that is challenging, to grow in my awareness and, I hope, to allow you in reading this to identify ways in which you can find strength and perhaps even comfort in discovering what prayer is for you. And in what ways you are in communication with and in relationship with the divine both within you and beyond you – and right beside you.

My journey starts with my father and his breath prayer and it continues with a host of friends of different traditions who have helped me to reframe my understanding of prayer and to incorporate new contemplative practices into my life. Some of us need a broader understanding than perhaps our traditions encourage to sense the divine, present in our lives. How do we find our connection with the divine in the ordinary moments that perhaps we do not realize are sacred? Our lives are filled with practices and patterns that are prayer. If we expand our understanding of prayer far beyond what we have always thought it was, our awareness will grow of that which is undefinable and limitless – and very present in our lives.

> In the ordinary we find the extraordinary.
> In ritual we find rest.
> In re-examining what is at our foundation,
> there we find ourselves and the divine as one.

Sabbath

Saturday was sabbath. Sunday was the most intense workday, not just for the berobed one in the pulpit but for the rest of us too. Each of us had our role in the fishbowl life, that of the minister's family. So Saturday was protected religiously. I looked forward all week to the line-up of Saturday morning cartoons, and my mother looked forward to the deep exhalation of that morning with as much anticipation. *Land of the Lost* was her favorite, the dad and two kids traveling back to the time of the dinosaurs. We chatted away through every show. Amazing that we actually followed anything that was happening in the episode. By the time *The Pink Panther* was on, my father was bringing us a chopped-up egg in a cup, as my mother and I lingered in bed for those precious hours. While, in my child's mind, cartoons and breakfast in bed was living the life, in retrospect I see the ritual of creating space that both my parents cherished on those sabbath mornings.

Allowing the space for our contemplative practices and maintaining a rhythm or some form of regularity is key. Nothing is wasted time. In fact, the time that some might call wasted is very likely the most precious heart of your contemplative practice. So I use the word ritual in the sense that we find a practice that has meaning. And that meaning connects you deeply to something grounding and foundational, that moves you forward into the world to do the work you do with a renewed awareness of intention.

When I was introduced to the teachings and wisdom of Thich Nhat Hanh, beloved Vietnamese Thiền Buddhist monk, I recognized in the first pages of his book these sabbath rituals of my parents. Thay, as his followers devotedly call him, recounts a meeting with a friend, Allen, who has two young children and, apparently, not a moment of time for himself, for his own work and centering practice. Allen teaches Thay however that when he reframed the time spent with his children and partner as his own time, not as a stepping stone to get to his 'real work' or personal endeavors, he found that he had unlocked the secret to unlimited time. Thay translates this into his well-known teaching on washing dishes.

> 'There are two ways to wash the dishes. The first is to wash the dishes in order to have clean dishes and the second is to wash the dishes in order to wash the dishes.'[3]

In my path of seeking spiritual grounding from the wise teachers of different traditions, I was transported back to Saturday morning cartoons. The gentle rhythm of these sabbath days that my parents set was nourishment for them and for me. For family. For rest. There was a feeling that time was unlimited and belonged to us. My parents were teaching me the life's work of Thich Nhat Hanh, embodied in a family's Saturday morning ritual.

As I look back on those precious sabbath mornings, I see those hours infused with prayer. Not time set aside for prayer, but prayer in time set aside.

Tending the Fire

My consuming fascination with staring into flames began with my granny's coal fire. It was a sacred ritual for her. Up before anyone else could hear her stirring, she struck a match to the pile of coals and twisted balls of newspaper that she had set the night before. Her shoulders curled forward as she kneeled before the lifeless black rocks, tilting her head to blow gently. Breath met spark, and the day began. Warmth to the house. Light to the dark room. Duty for the matriarch. Comfort to a family cradled by this ritual. The warning was not to get too close. Chilblains might ensue. But the invitation was always to sit, be still, stoke, feed, keep watch – hold wonder and reverence for the fire. My life as a pastor's kid was filled with formal times and locations for prayer, but the daily simplicity and necessity of my granny's practice revealed a much more practical form of prayer.

Did she know she was praying? Perhaps not. Did I look at her bent frame, humbled and reverent, and recognize it as prayer? Not at the time. But now, without a doubt, I know that those focused morning moments were part of her contemplative practice. It was rooted in duty and awe. It was intimate and personal. In the hushed moments before the day began, she met the divine. Although her life was pitted with the marks of loss and grief, poverty and heartache, war and emigration, she met her maker every morning. There in the glowing embers and the leaping flames was something more powerful than she was – with the strength to consume as well as to warm. Nevertheless she was not consumed. She held herself in right relationship with her God.

Nec tamen consumebatur. Long before I taught the language, these words in Latin were etched in my mind. A stone carving of the burning bush on the fireplace in my father's office at church. *Nevertheless it was not consumed.* Sure, this emblem of the Church of Scotland was an appropriate carving to have in a minister's office, a Scottish immigrant in Philadelphia. Funny even, on the fireplace. But I imagine my father must have stopped and considered those words each day when he went to work. To step into the role of leading a congregation, of upholding the creeds and confessions, of caring and counseling, but also of provoking people to live their lives grounded in the call to divine justice and love, surely it would be easy to be consumed. But here's the tricky part, he stayed authentic to his own personal practices every day. And in that way, I am confident, he was not consumed.

His intimate and personal prayer took the form of his daily practices, just like my granny's. He sang with the birds, he wrote poetry in front of his Buddha statue, he kneaded bread and shared it with those he loved. I am sure the work that I do now was grounded in what I learned by his side. Interfaith Alignment is an organization that offers contemplative practices from a variety of traditions. The intention is to offer to those who seek peace an array of options for how to be in contemplative prayer. To expand the understanding of prayer for those who have felt it limiting or lacking. We hold the hope that if we can embrace the traditions of others and open our hearts and minds, then surely the work of pursuing justice for all people will be the natural consequence. Some practices feel familiar and others are very new. Sometimes a practice from another tradition feels more appropriate for us than one from our own. As you journey through this book, you will meet some of the people and practices that have been a part of Alignment.

It began with observing the simple rituals of my family. The reverence, awe and respect that accompanied them – all things that are so necessary when we engage in interfaith relationships. And by finding what grows authentically from the daily practices of our own life.

> May we not be consumed by what we think is the right way to pray.
> Consumed by expectations.
> Consumed by that which limits what is limitless.
> May the light of the divine fire illumine our way.

Practice

LOVING WORDS

Sabbath, from the Hebrew root letters Shin - Bet - Tav (שׁנת) carries the meaning of stopping, ceasing, resting, and is usually associated with the day when we disengage from our regular daily work for prayer, study, or other soul-nourishing time. Rabbi Marcia Prager teaches that on Shabbat, by refraining from our work in the material world, we can concentrate on personal and communal spiritual growth and thus pattern our days on a divine rhythm. In traditional Jewish settings, no materially transformative work is done, even the driving of a car to the synagogue or the turning on of lights. But in more secular settings, we can use the term more loosely to mean some time 'off'. You'll recognize the same S-B-T root in the word sabbatical. But I offer a simple reminder that sabbath does not need to be defined by a month away from work or a weekend day for worship. Sabbath can be present in every moment of daily activity. Imagine that beautiful meal before you, so lovingly prepared and delightfully displayed. Eaten to fuel our bodies; eaten because it's time to eat; or eaten to distract us from some other pain. S-B-T. Stop for a moment and look at the next forkful. Take yourself to all of the hands that went into bringing that food to that fork. From the farmers to the factory workers. See its colors and textures. Taste it anew. A simple pause in the midst of the ritual of repast is a taste of sabbath. It is prayer.

RETHINK

Rituals can be found in the ordinary actions of our daily life. Perhaps instead of a prayer to begin your meal, you pray as you are eating.

REFRAME

Look again at the moments that bring you into more focused alignment with peace and love in your life. Times that may seem like you are doing nothing may, in fact, be important times of rest and renewal, of grounding and connection.

REIMAGINE

Incorporate a practice in your life of ritual and rest from the Jewish tradition of sabbath-keeping and the Buddhist tradition of mindfulness. Find these in the moments and movements already part of your daily and weekly routine.

Chapter 2
Creating Sacred Space

Practice seeing the sacred in the ordinary
Set aside in space and time
Or right in the middle of it all

Ordinary Rituals that Create Sacred Space

The bedside alarm, anticipated but still always surprising, sets in motion a series of tasks that unfold without much conscious thought process. From the brushing of teeth to the feeding of the dog, the morning could perhaps be the most densely populated field for us to mine for ordinary rituals. Our brains are barely functioning but we know exactly the motions and routines that make up those first waking hours. Perhaps your day begins with a few words or readings or movements of centering gratitude. A salutation to the sun. A devotional verse. A journal entry. It is, however, very likely that it sounds like a dream to have the space for that type of routine. Instead it is a flurry of bags to be packed and clothes to be chosen and feet that must get out the door. Whatever the circumstances, recognizing the motions is the first step to creating sacred space.

Heidi Barr, poet, wellness coach, author of creative nonfiction, and keen observer of the patterns of daily living, calls us to take a moment to observe the unobserved. Those tasks that fill our lives, whether from necessity or habit, that carve paths of ritual throughout our waking hours. The ceremonies of the ordinary – a phrase she borrows from Kent Nerburn in her book *Collisions of Earth and Sky*. To find the sacredness in the ordinary opens the space for us to find holiness in our own being. To find the divine entrenched in the very stuff that makes us who we are. 'What can be uncovered by peering deeply into the ordinary actions of our days and discovering the rituals that already exist inside them.'[4] All it takes is a moment to notice how to create sacred space.

Heidi Barr prompts us to think about a chore during which we usually 'just go through the motions' and to transfer our awareness to ritualizing the task. To think about the simple shift enabled by recognizing the chore as a sacred moment, something that holds meaning and the possibility of being life-giving. The dreaded vacuuming that consumes minutes I wish I could get back. The dog hair that seems to come from ten dogs living in my house on any given day when there is only my one sweet pup. The shift from the nuisance of it all to the satisfying sound of a space being cleared, the hum of the machine, and the companionship of the one whose shedding body creates the task. A ritual not sacred until we make it so. Heidi uplifts Robin Wall Kimmerer's teaching in *Braiding Sweetgrass*, the marriage of the mundane and the sacred, in her own prompting to create ceremony from the ordinary movements of our living. An invitation not only to carve space for those sacred spaces in our day, but to recognize each movement, each moment, as holy in its ordinariness.

Sitting in Sacred Space

Enter the door as if the floor within were gold
All of jewels of wealth untold
As if the choir in robes of fire were singing here
Nor shout. Nor rush. But hush. For God is here.

I read this poem every Sunday as I was growing up. Settling into my seat right under the pulpit where my father would preach, I engaged in my own ritual. Mother to my left, brother to my right. Red velvet pew cushion jabbing my leg with stray horse hairs underneath. I lifted the card from where it was tucked into a metal pew rack, edges warped from my weekly use, and I read this poem. Pleased with myself that I had it memorized, but reading it anyway to check and make sure I had it right. All part of the ritual. I am quite sure I couldn't have articulated it as a child, but I think I was captivated by the internal rhymes and the images it conjured, but mostly it filled me with wonder about the sacredness of the space. It was a space set apart for me to know God was there. It instilled in me a sense of reverence for coming into the sanctuary, to sit in silence in the moments before the service began, to imagine bejeweled floors and a fire-robed choir. Reverence and wonder took root.

To this day flying buttresses and stained-glass windows flip the sacred space switch for me. The heavier the *porta sancta*, the better. Set my feet on a marble floor, and I'm putty.

Eventually, however, I came to know God's presence in spaces and times that had nothing to do with church and even beyond things that represented splendor. It took a seminary degree to make me comfortable with the fact that I could be in relationship with God outside of my own tradition as well. I could find God's presence in the chanting of Hindu mantras and Islamic nasheeds. God was not limited to correct practice or time-honored theology or even gothic naves. My understanding of the divine was enriched by coming to see how unlimited God was, without boundaries, living and pulsing in the hearts of people who did not even call God by name – the one I knew or any name at all. Every space where I found connection to divine presence became holy ground.

Zach Freidhof, Troubador of Peace from the Teton Mountains of Wyoming, reminds participants in his kirtan sessions that the very spot in which you are right now is holy ground. The very moment that you are setting aside is a sacred space. I sit in my swivel office chair, logged into Zoom, for a session of Interfaith Alignment. Thirty minutes set aside each week as an intentional sacred space, to create connections for those who are seeking peace. Zach leads those assembled online in chants of his own composition from the great Hindu mantras.

Where I sit is holy, holy is the ground
Forest, mountain, river, listen to the sound

While Zach chants these words over the next eight minutes, I am recognizing the ordinariness of my chair, neither carved nor velvet-lined, but bought from IKEA. And its holiness. Where I sit is holy. Because I have set apart this time as sacred space.

Listen to the ordinary sounds of creation and recognize them as holy. Remember that even the chair in our den or the hum of the dishwasher, even those, in the recognition of their ordinariness, are conveyors of sacred space for us, because we are present in them. And we are alive in them. And in our living and in our being is the divine within and beside us.

'God comes to us disguised as our life.'[5]

The Posture of Prayer

Knees humbled to the ground and forehead kissing the earth. Chin dropped to the chest and fingers entwined. Legs in lotus and eyes gently focused downward. For many, creating a sacred space involves assuming a particular posture. One of humility. Or of opening. Or of meditative stillness. A US survey on prayer from a project called American Prayer Wrap[6] indicates that for most people prayer does not, in fact, involve any of these postures. This opens up a beautiful truth: prayer is a part of the ordinary spaces and moments of our daily lives. Even when time is not set aside, even when postures are not assumed, prayer comes and lives with us, as close as our every breath.

Praying in the Shower

Surely it is not a coincidence that prayer flows easily when water washes over us. Spiritual practices from Muslim, Bahá'í, Hindu, Christian, Jewish and Indigenous traditions, among others, centralize water as the source of the divine. Purifying and renewing, it is the vital energy of life itself and, as we learn from Quranic teachings, the epiphany of the divine qualities.

My children, raised in the Christian tradition, grew up alongside their best friends who were Hindu. When sleepovers began, we noticed right away the difference in our showering practices. At first it seemed like a simple difference in family preference. But as our friendship deepened, and we grew to share our faith traditions, from baptisms to pujas, we thought more intentionally about the difference in our interaction with water. Our Hindu friends cleansed their body at night before going to sleep, just as they seek to shed the maya, the illusion, that ties them to this life. We greeted the new day by immersing ourselves in the flowing water, just as we live in the promise of life renewed. A simple cultural difference in showering habits, but perhaps a powerful reminder that although we may pray in different ways, we all seek connection to a life-giving source.

The American Prayer Wrap survey records that 25% of surveyed prayers note that their prayers happen in the shower. Whether it is the impact of the flowing water that opens our hearts and minds to the practice or the fact that this is time set apart for relative peace and solitude, the shower seems a natural sacred space. It both incorporates and expands the postures most commonly recognized in prayer. And we come to this space most vulnerable, most free, our voices most resonant.

Praying in the Car

More surprising results perhaps note that although 46% of people surveyed pray in their place of worship, 61% pray in their car. How utterly symbolic of the important connection between prayer and action. Perhaps it calls to mind Henri Nouwen's familiar reminder,

> *Prayer and action ... can never be seen as contradictory or mutually exclusive. Prayer without action grows into powerless pietism, and action without prayer degenerates into questionable manipulation.*[7]

When we get in our car, we are going somewhere. Certainly there are times when we drive for the sake of driving, but as part of our daily practice, more likely there is a destination in sight. There are schedules and deadlines. There are routine routes and expected traffic. There are frustrations and detours. And apparently, there is prayer. Again the survey opens for us an awareness. It is in the midst of this very business that we remember. Our communication with our source, with spirit, is in the messiness of life.

Praying at Work

And ultimately prayer is in the very work that we have been called to do in this life. Of the 39% of those surveyed who attest to praying at work, it seems as if some are seeking intentional space, whereas others find prayer clinging to them as they walk throughout their day.

I visited Bryn Mawr College's Student Life and Wellness Building when it was newly opened, where staff supporting Religious and Spiritual Life are located. Asheq Fazlullah, the Muslim student advisor, showed me the prayer space created in the new building with a wudu station for ablutions. They have designed the workplace with the understanding that, of course, there will be prayer during the workday. It is common now to find prayer rooms in hospitals and airports, but the sad truth is that most workplaces do not assume that there are those who will need a place to pray during the workday.

Perhaps when we think of prayer, we situate our image in a sacred space. A presumed posture. A room set aside. But when we live a life of prayer that is as close as every breath, we find our sacred spaces in the ordinary workings of our lives. We find our prayers are the gentle ways in which we make connection with the ordinary. So yes, we hope that our schools and workplaces will be better at providing room and time and support for those who require a space set aside for prayer. At the same time, we can reframe and reimagine what defines a space as sacred.

Expanding the Posture of Prayer

In worship services from many different traditions, prayer is structured. Types of prayer are labeled. Times for prayer are scheduled. Words of prayer are composed. Places for prayer are set aside. But prayer that takes us beyond these boundaries expands our connection to the divine, and perhaps from there deepens our understanding of the limitless presence of spirit in our lives.

During a brief time of my life when I thought following in my father's actual footsteps might be the right path for me, I was leading a congregation in a traditional Presbyterian worship service. Before walking down the aisle, berobed in black myself, actually in my retailored father's robes, I prayed silently for peace, strength and clarity. Then I took my spot. No longer were ministers kneeling at the communion table in the back as he had. Positioned at the lectern, microphone on, standing some twenty feet away from the nearest congregant, I prompted the congregation to sit at the appropriate time. Some slumped their bodies a little lower during this final time of intercessory prayer at the end of the hour-long service. Some just lowered their chins a bit closer to their hearts. This was the big prayer. We had raised our songs of praise, confessed our sins, and been assured of God's grace. We had dedicated our offerings, financial and otherwise. But this was the long prayer at the end. With final words of gratitude for God's presence among us, we held the concerns of our communities, near and far.

I pray rather slowly, too slowly for the rhythm of this traditional worship service and the slot allotted for this final prayer. I pause between petitions. Not moments of silence, but pause for the breath to enter. When the congregation joins me in the Lord's Prayer at the end, I can see that my pace has been too slow for them. I have to match their speed in darting to the finish line. And the glory forever. Amen. At the end of the service I was thanked for the good job I had done by some, but was also given the feedback that it could have been shorter, faster, fewer pauses.

Now granted, this is a congregation that watched me grow up as a little girl hiding under the robes of my father. But when someone congratulates me on 'doing a good job', I feel as if I have failed. I have not welcomed them into conversation with the divine. Instead I have adjusted my prayer to fit into the allotted space. I have sped up my pace and shortened my pauses to match the rhythm of the congregation. Have I, however, found a way for them not just to be bystanders in my communion with spirit, but participants in prayer? Can they lift their heads from prayer and still see spirit swirling in the sacred space of the sanctuary?

I remember as a child folding my body in two during this long prayer, my forehead touching my knees, and listening only to the sound of my father's voice. Then awakened by the *amen*, I blinked open my eyes, stretched back to upright, and flipped through the hymnal for the last part before coffee hour. It was not the words he said that held me in prayer, but the sound and the posture. The pace and the presence.

Later on that day, the day I did the good job praying, I thought about my intention. I had hoped to transport the pray-ers into a more expansive sacred space, one that carried us beyond the sacred structure of wood and marble to the actual sacred spaces of creation. To experience the peace and strength and clarity found in God's creation. I imagined that instead of saying the words, 'You may be seated,' I had flung open the doors and walked the congregation to the nearest park.

What I prayed that day:

> *We pray for peace.*
> *Peace for those who are at war.*
> *For those who cannot keep their children safe.*
> *For those who live their lives in fear.*
> *Fear on the streets where they live.*
> *And fear in their own homes.*
> *For those tormented by the very thought of living another day.*
> *May we see them, merciful God, as you already do.*
> *May we know your peace in these moments of prayer*
> *and be vessels, filled to overflowing*
> *that your peace might spill from us*
> *like the cascading waters of your good earth.*

How I would expand that prayer:

> *Put your hands in the cool cascade of the waterfall.*
> *As the water slips through your fingers, watch its path.*
> *Downstream it slides over rocks, and ripples in collected pools.*
> *Knowing not where it is headed, it continues.*
> *Upstream it is ever-flowing. It is unmeasured. Its depth unknown.*
> *Its cadence, however, steady and sure.*
> *It is peace for the fearful heart and the tormented mind in its surety and constancy.*
> *Put your hands in the cascade and know the peace of God.*

What I prayed:

> *We pray for strength*
> *For those who wake in the morning not knowing*
> *in what direction to turn.*
> *For those who crave what harms them.*
> *For those in pain, physical, and mental, and spiritual pain.*

> *For those who have experienced loss that has left them empty.*
> *For those who are not free to share their true identity,*
> *who they know they truly are.*
> *May we hold them, as you already do.*
> *May we know the strength that comes from you*
> *that we might be their rock,*
> *that your strength might steady us*
> *like the majestic mountains of your good earth.*

How I would expand that prayer:

> *Set your feet on the ground and walk.*
> *Take the road less traveled.*
> *Feel the incline of the path rising to hill,*
> *your heartbeat quickening like new life forming.*
> *And stop to put your hands in the grass.*
> *Feel that which supports our very existence,*
> *which underlies our shelter,*
> *which produces our sustenance, which teaches us of growth.*
> *Sense the support in every step.*
> *Climb the mountain of what lies before you*
> *and know the strength of God.*

What I prayed:

> *We pray for clarity*
> *For those who are in positions of power.*
> *In our city, our nation, in every nation.*
> *Those who make decisions that ripple down to those living in poverty,*
> *those who are unaware of the part they play in systemic racism,*
> *all of us who cannot see how we are harming this planet*
> *with our waste and our consumption.*
> *May we all be held in the light of your unquenchable love.*
> *May we know the clarity that comes*
> *when we set our hearts and minds at rest in you*
> *that your light might lift us like the cloud of witnesses*
> *that surrounds us even now.*

How I would expand that prayer:

> *Hold your face to meet the sun.*
> *The light that filters even through eyes fully closed.*
> *The shapes and colors that emerge when you look away.*
> *Images before unseen.*
> *And listen for what surrounds you.*
> *Chirps and crunches and rustles that were there unnoticed*
> *when we did not make the space to listen.*
> *You are surrounded in the light of the divine,*
> *in the clarity of what is present and yet unseen.*
> *And you have been in prayer.*
> *Connected to the spirit of creation in peace and strength*
> *and a clarity that comes from expanding*
> *the narrow spaces of our practice.*

Amen. Ashe. Aho. Shanti.

Practice

LOVING WORDS

The English word *sacred* is a very clear derivative, in form and function, from the Latin word *sacer*, used for things that were set apart for special use, dedicated for the divine. It is the root of everything from *sacrifice* to *sacrilege*. But what makes that bone at the end of our spine so special? Attempts at uncovering the significance of the *sacrum* are wide-ranging. Greeks and Romans thought that it was the temple of the life-producing organs. The Egyptians used the bone as an amulet to signify strength and permanence. Islamic writings mark it as the first bone to be created in the body, tying in closely with Jewish Talmudic writings that recognize it as indestructible, and therefore the part of the body from which resurrection will come. I like this thought, that what we set apart as sacred is linked to something as common in us as our butt, and which also points in the direction of giving and renewing life.[8]

What would have made this just perfect would be if the S-C-R consonants at the base of this word were somehow linked through its Indo-European roots to the Sanskrit *chakra* and the sacral chakra as the seat of creativity and emotion, sexuality, and connection to others, but alas.

It is also a word that is sometimes mistranslated. The Latin term *os sacrum* is a translation of the Greek term for the bone, *hieron osteon*. The problem arises when a word holds a semantic domain with a range of possible translations. Here *hieron* could be sacred/holy or large/great/steady/magnificent. Once a translator chooses one translation from the range, it sets the term in one direction when it could, in fact, have been heading in another. Take, for example, the Hebrew word for young woman, *almah* (who was likely unmarried, and therefore likely a virgin), translated into Greek as *parthenos* (think Athena Parthenos, the unmarried, not-in-need-of-a-man goddess of war and wisdom). And then the subsequent Latin translation of *parthenos* as *virgo*, leading us to a belief of an immaculate conception of Jesus. How different would Christianity have been if we had instead associated Mary with the strength in mind and might of a woman who could raise a child on her own?

Perhaps you understand now that by Loving Words, I mean I love words and how they shape that which is deeply rooted in our systems. So take the word sacred and hold it close, and find those sacred spaces that are both ordinary and life-giving.

RETHINK

Sacred space is wherever you create it. Outside of houses of faith. Outside. Simply by assuming a posture.

REFRAME

Look again at the ordinary moments, the ordinary spaces, and the ordinary actions of your life as life-giving. Think of space in terms of location, time and posture. Are there places that take your breath away? Are there moments when you can take a breath more deeply? Is there a way of standing or sitting or being that brings alignment to your body, mind and spirit.

REIMAGINE

Identify a space that has nothing to do with a traditional house of faith, one in which holiness is palpable. In which a person of any tradition or background would feel both at peace and inspired. Where you could be in sacred communion with your neighbor and your creator.

Chapter 3

Becoming a Vessel

Practice being a vessel
Filled with the love of the one who made you
Sacred in your ordinariness

Emptied Space

The night was deeply steeped in silence and stillness, except for the rhythmic rocking of the chair. I held a precious new life snuggled into my neck. The comfort of having him so close to my body when I had carried him within for so long was too alluring. It was well past the time when I should have gently made the transfer to the crib, to catch what fleeting moments of sleep might be left in the night.

I was too tired to move.

I was too tired to think.

And so we rocked.

Soon a poem appeared from nowhere, its meter matching the cadence of the chair. It came not from conscious thought, not from any source that I recognized or could identify.

Rhyming, rhythmic, expressive, resonant, playful, complete.

I had the overwhelming realization that the poem was created from utter depletion. From entering a state where there was nothing in that moment except unfathomable love. And I was simply a vessel. My mind had not searched for words. I had not written poetry for years. There was no intention or inclination. It just was. I did not write it down, but I recited it every morning to the precious soul who opened his eyes to greet the new day. Nor do I write the poem down here because the words are not mine to share. They belong to my son. Now, more than three decades later, I remember every word, and I recall that feeling of being so empty that the gift of creation entered.

What does it mean to be a vessel? Surely there is a monumental shift when one transitions from being a physical vessel for a life growing within to becoming a caretaker and then ultimately a bystander in that life. A shift that reveals the delicate boundary between loss and new life. It does not, however, take an experience of childbirth to access our capacity to be a spiritual vessel. But it just might take that experience of allowing ourselves to become depleted. Devoid of all the noise and activity that separates us from the divinity that dwells in the depths of our being. That depletion may come from grief or loss or from separating ourselves from ego. Or it may come from trained contemplative practice that opens our hearts and minds. Either way, the experience undoubtedly creates space for us to be one with the divine, to access a well from which we ourselves and others might draw sustenance.

As my family of children grew, those moments of nighttime exhaustion became a center of spiritual retreat for me. I found poem after poem appearing in that space, the precious weight of a drooling baby on one shoulder, the familiar rhythm of the rocking chair keeping beat. No computer. No pen and paper. Just the emptiness allowing pure connection.

One morning I wrote down what had materialized during the night and saw that the poem contained two voices. My voice speaking to my infant daughter and my father's voice speaking to me. The same words. My father who had died fourteen years before – who came into that space and gave me words to give my daughter. They were set to the tune *O Waly Waly*, an old English melody, and sung at my daughter's baptism by a full choir and congregation and resounding pipe organ. And then sung again at my mother's memorial service, the words now given from her beloved to her. Where was I in this process? I was the vessel. I was the empty space into which something that I could not comprehend had entered. I questioned whether I had arrived at this sense of connection by mere chance. Had exhaustion played tricks with my mind? But in later studies of Buddhist practices of emptying the mind, I thought that perhaps this had simply been my conduit to meditative practice. Practice that connected me intimately to the experience of creation.

I began to seek practices that would take me to this space without the exhaustion – that contemplative space that Cassidy Hall, in her book *Queering Contemplation*, reminds us is concerned with both attention and emptiness.⁹ Throughout this book you will find the ways in which my understanding of prayer is tied to these practices of seeking deep connection. The spaces materialized through experiences that enabled me to recognize the divine that is rooted in the core of who I am myself – even during the times when I felt the most self-doubt, even self-loathing. I was not seeking God in a holy house of faith but in the dark moments of the night and within my own being.

A long journey later my work shifted to facilitating these experiences for others. Creating a community where people of any tradition or no tradition from anywhere around the world could come together online to practice creating sacred space. Interfaith Alignment was born:

> *an international interfaith community of understanding and practice that is grounded in the experience of the divine, that bridges and expands individuals' own faith traditions, and that deepens individuals' spiritual lives and connections to the divine and one another; to discover and expand resources for interfaith contemplative practice; to thereby undergird work for justice in the world.*¹⁰

Every week for thirty minutes, whoever comes across the link joins us. The group is different every week. Some people are regulars, some come only once in a while, but the overwhelming majority of people who participate are seeking sacred space. Whether they are depleted by grief or loss or abuse, or they feel disconnected from community or perhaps the tradition in which they were raised, or their hearts are simply open to embracing new practices, new ways of knowing and understanding divine presence in their lives, the people who attend Interfaith Alignment find new and sometimes very unexpected ways to be in prayer.

Clay Pots

A lump of clay thrown onto the potter's wheel becomes a vessel. Lester Morris, tech consultant by day, recognizes his time at the wheel as his spiritual practice. He invited the participants of Alignment into his basement ceramics studio virtually for a session of contemplative practice. The pots and bowls that Lester shaped during our time together became vessels for far more than anyone anticipated.

One of the main intentions of Alignment is the recognition of the sacred in the ordinary. We look for the presence of the divine in the workings of our life that both center us and move us forward, that connect us to the divinity that exists at the depths of our existence. And the divinity that challenges us to step beyond our own circumstances, to connect with those who are different from us but also deeply a part of our human experience. We find our practices of prayer in the routines and rituals that are already a part of daily life. The ordinary, set apart in the very recognition of it, becomes the sacred. And so it is with Lester's wheel spinning in meditative practice that yields a vessel. A symbol of our shaping, our abundance, and our voids.

There is nothing much more common than a pot. A bowl. That which holds our sustenance. Which fills our tables and our cupboards. From which we bathe. And into which we pour that which no longer serves. Dredged up from the sea after 2500 years, a pot that carried oil or grain or wine from Roman transport speaks across the millennia – the earth made into vessel is part of the universal human experience. But when we step back to view the creation of the pot, that is when the divine enters. The hands of the potter become the hands of the creator, and we the clay shaped by our encounter.

The Hebrew scriptures are replete with references to the potter and the clay, to pots and vessels. None more obvious perhaps than the words of the prophet Isaiah. *But now, O Lord, you are our father, we are the clay, and you our potter, and we all are the work of your hand* (Isaiah 64:8). The prophet's role is to be the voice of God for the people and the voice of the people for God. The voice enabling divinity and humanity to be in relationship. Perhaps this reminds us that we are potters too. In recognizing the divine act of creation in the shaping of the pot on the wheel, we are reminded of the divinity that abides at the core of our being.

The prophet Jeremiah who cries out at the time of the destruction of Jerusalem by the Babylonians speaks to the presence of the divine in the depths of human experience. We are assured that new life is not only a possibility but is the expectation when we place ourselves in the presence of the divine. *Then I went down to the potter's house, and there he was, making something on the wheel. But the vessel that he was making of clay was spoiled in the hand of the potter; so he remade it into another vessel, as it pleased the potter to make* (Jer 18:3-4).

In the Islamic tradition, Allah breathes into the clay form of a bird that the prophet Isa makes. The healing potential of the prophet comes from the will and permission of the one who makes the clay a living form – a symbol of that which came from the earth and which will fly to the outer reaches of creation. Through the breath of the divine and the hands of the prophet-potter, new life is given. From the Quran: *Allah will say, when you designed from clay [what was] like the form of a bird with my permission, then you breathed into it and it became a bird with my permission.* (Surah Al-Ma'idah - 110)

Not only the earthen material of the pot but also the function of the pot is foundationally common to our daily lives. In sacred ritual, we often see the ordinary clay pot as the point at which the divine comes into relationship with us. Madhvi Subrahmanian, founding member and co-curator of Indian Ceramics Triennale in Mumbai, in presenting her work at the International Academy of Ceramics, writes of the Hindu use of earthen pots in ceremony. 'The pot plays an important role in rituals where Gods and Goddess [sg] are projected to descend into the *ghata* or the pot during a ritual, which then becomes the intermediary between the devotee and the deity.'[11] It symbolizes both abundance and the void. The overflowing pot symbolizes fertility, and the empty pot represents the vastness of the cosmos.

Adam Posner studies the sacred rituals of African-Pan-American religious systems through the lens of his work with clay. Through his fascinating piece *To Serve the Divine*, he discusses the use of ordinary clay pots, cooking vessels for instance, that become a part of sacred ritual. He says that often the way they are adorned or filled or decorated leads to the view that the ordinary has become sacred, that the pots themselves are being worshipped. But he makes clear that the widespread practice among African and African-Caribbean traditions is that the pots are 'temporary seats or housing for the divine essence; in other words the pot is not itself sacred, but rather it contains the spiritual force.'[12]

As Lester Morris threw mounds of unshaped clay onto his wheel, participants in Alignment's session, Creative Clay, spent the half hour in meditative reflection. They engaged in their own spiritual practice as they sat in witness to Lester's. Even without touching the clay ourselves, the practice was a shared one. The Zoom chat filled with messages of wonder, transformation, nourishment and hope. The significance of the gentle touch to the clay that produces ripples of change allowed some to remember how connection to the divine can be imperceptible. How there is a pattern of energy and then pause that balances the interaction. One participant noted:

> *I'm remembering all the times when I have felt like a simple lump of clay, times when I may lack confidence or think I'm nothing special ... and there have been so many other times that I've allowed myself to be formed and opened, lovingly cared for and molded. Also remembering how many people in my life have been a vessel, a container for me.*

Lester's vessels had become a vessel for our contemplative practice. The ordinary became the sacred. The practice of creating the common vessel becomes the space into which the divine enters.

The Dancer as Vessel

Savita Singh prays through dance and chant. Her prayers tell the stories of humanity's interactions with divinity both within and beyond. With every articulate gesture of hands and eyes and feet, the dancer becomes the vessel not just for the story but for the divinity herself.

The dancer conveys awe at the beauty of Shakti and the feelings of radiance that she evokes within. The dancer asks again and again for the benevolence of the mother and the power of Shakti to overcome *maya*, illusion. But the dancer is also an embodiment of the power and grace and beauty of the *devi*, the goddess herself. It is an expression of the connection known in Hindu tradition of the inseparability of the divine and human.

Ya devi sarva-bhuteshu vishnu-mayeti sadbita Namas tasyai, namas tasyai, namas tasyai namo namah

To that devi who lives in all beings in the form of strength
of consciousness
of mother
of kindness, mercy
of forgiveness, tolerance
of intelligence, wisdom
of knowledge
of memory
of faith, reverence
of devotion
of peace, serenity, calmness, tranquility
of prosperity
Salutations to her, salutations, salutations again and again.
To that devi who exists in all beings. Salutations to her, salutations, salutations again and again.

Savita Singh hails from several generations of Hindu priests. Growing up in Guyana, interfaith engagement was an ordinary part of her life. She did not have to seek opportunities to live and work and pray with those of other traditions. She lived the rhythm of Muslim, Christian and Hindu worship and celebration. Her traditions, from what she eats to how she prays, have been woven from the organic interfaith existence of this life. She serves in the Hindu community and other faith communities to bring awareness to the Hindu way of life, its traditions, beliefs and practices, but in doing so she strives to unify and not to divide with her religious beliefs. Savita's belief is that divinity lives within us. We are the vessel that is also inseparable from what it contains.

What Spills Out

There is a story that surfaces on social media from time to time. I first heard it from my homiletics professor, Karyn Wiseman, who takes very seriously the responsibility to both challenge her students and be a source of support and pastoral care for them, as she trains them to do for others. The story was a reminder that in caring for others we must be sure of what fills our own cups.

As it goes, a person holding a cup of coffee is bumped into by another. The coffee spills out. The question posed to the listener: why did coffee spill out of the cup? The usual answer: because someone was clumsy, or rude, or in too much of a hurry to notice their surroundings. No, the answer with the message is: coffee spilled out because there was coffee in the cup. Had there been tea in the cup, tea would have spilled out, etc. The learning: when life bumps us around, what spills out is that with which we have filled our vessels.

There was a dark, dark time in my life when my vessel felt completely empty. I had lost a community, a job, family and friends, as well as my feeling of self-worth and purpose. My understanding of God had shifted so monumentally that I did not feel able to turn to the traditional prayers on which I had been raised. I remember laughing (the only laugh that came out for a long time) at my therapist who said, 'Is there something in the Bible that would be comforting for you to read right now?' No, there wouldn't be. But there was someone who was a vessel of divine love when mine was empty. She repeated the words to me: 'You are strong; you are loved; you are beautiful; you are enough.' She repeated them so that they would be my mantra. A prayer in the middle of the night when sleep would not come. She took me away for a few days to get out of my house. She found out when the pool in the hotel would be empty and made me swim from one end to the other, repeating: 'You are strong. You are loved. You are beautiful. You are enough.'

Sometimes she would text the phrases which arrived on my phone one by one.

You are strong. Send.
You are loved. Send.
You are beautiful. Send.
You are enough. Send.

It took as much out of her to support me through my desolation as suffering it took out of me. She recognized through it all that she was the vessel for this message, and that she was filling my cup. So that when I was jostled by wave after wave of what I thought I would never survive, this is what would spill out. She was prophet and pastor. She was a conduit for divine grace. She was a vessel.

Whether our empty spaces come from joyful births or devastating loss, whether we are the clay or the potter, whether our vessels are for sacred ritual or daily food, they hold the possibility of meeting the divine. And spilling out of that vessel will be a prayer. It may have words. It may have only feelings. Perhaps just tears. But without a doubt, it will be a prayer.

Immanent Light

Where do you sit,
Divine that is within me?
In the seat of my heart or mind or gut
Where fear grips
And thoughts swirl unchecked
And love swells unbounded,
Is that where you sit, my light?

Have you taken up space beside
In the tears that are about to spill
And the bowels about to split?
Do you wrap yourself around each strand of DNA
A coating balm and antidote to pain?

Do you come within invited
Called for presence in the soul
The parts that are unknown
that animate?
Is it in the gaps where hope resides
That spirit fills
sand poured among the rocks
Completing us?

Or are you one with me
Not around, between, among

But of the very one
Begotten not called
Light of light
The suffering wounds
The radiant joy
The fire that burns for justice
All.

Prayers are whispered in the hush
Not to an ear all-hearing, all-knowing
But to echoed reverberations within each cell
of what makes me,
a vessel of divine light.

Practice

LOVING WORDS

For you etymology-loving folx, yes, we are technically one big living system of vessels. The word *vessel* derives from the Latin *vascellum*, hence our blood vessels are part of our vascular system. To the Romans it was either a diminutive vase or the ship, the vessel that transported the smaller vessels of oil or grain. Focus for a moment on the notion of movement that is so embedded in the term vessel when we identify it with blood vessels and ships, conduits. For me this is helpful, because when I think about being a vessel and the emptying that precedes the filling and spilling out, I can easily get stuck in the image of something deep and hollow. But it is a term filled with movement. Our vessels do get filled, and our cups runneth over. Even in the emptiest of times, it may be helpful to visualize the image of the vessel filling to the brim with divine love, so much that it spills over.

RETHINK ...

prayer as the vessel and the contents of the vessel, the making, the emptying and the filling.

REFRAME

The words and images and thoughts and emotions that materialize from times of depletion. Their very appearance may be the gift of prayer coming to you. And it may look like a poem or a drawing or it may be words of support offered by a friend.

REIMAGINE

There may be a time when you feel emptied, whether from exhaustion or from despair or from the practice of meditation. Can you imagine allowing the emptiness to be? There is a space there where you and the divine are one.

Chapter 4

Knowing Your Limits

Practice knowing your limits
If the last peak is too much
You have not failed
You have left more for tomorrow

False Summits

The false summit has got to be one of the most frustrating things in life. When the climb is steep and the footing unsure, the promise that in ten more steps you will have reached the summit might be all the fuel that is left. Then it's another ten. And unfortunately another. There is a hill in Scotland, Dumgoyne, that looks like an elephant in repose. Its scooped trunk is the slope that marks the end of the range of hills called the Campsies. Although it is a hill-walking short climb, it is steep. And gravelly. With extensive patches of shale on the path where one step forward can lead to an annoying slide backward. And it is riddled with false summits to get to the head of the elephant. Perhaps they are its grassy jaw bone and cheek and ear. Not wanting to look weak next to my fitness instructor cousin who can run up this hill, I took it all in stride. Ten steps at a time. Sometimes twelve back, but another ten, and another ten.

Then I had an overwhelming sense that I should stop. Not reach the peak. Not achieve the goal. Not listen to the encouragement that we're almost there. But listen to something within me that said stop. I was perched with one leg anchored straight down and the other knee bent up to my chest, ready to slide, not secure, but I stopped. I waited there for twenty minutes with the experience of not making it. And there it was, as with the rocking baby at night, a poem that materialized with the wind that was pressing me into the side of the hill. I pulled out my phone and wrote it in a note. It's gone now. Deleted at some point. But the memory of the experience is vivid. I didn't make it to the top. And there, in that space of non-completion, came a form of wholeness that changed my perspective. What if I become aware of my limits? What if accomplishment and achievement are not where my spirit finds shalom. I have been plagued by the urge towards achievement my whole life. I inherited the blessing and curse of the to-do list from my father, who used to trick himself in the same way I still do. He would start his list with tasks that he had already completed, creating the illusion of accomplishment right from the start. It translated to rock-solid study habits, an organized schedule, and a well-oiled machine. As an educator and lifelong learner, I focus on being better, learning more, honing my skills, setting new goals. All good practices. But a few years ago my daughter, recently graduated from college, sat me down and said, 'Look, you don't need to take any more classes or earn any more degrees or have any more jobs. Start just enjoying.' She was calling me on the carpet to practice what I preach. She was calling me into the sacred space of non-achievement.

Not long after her call to slow down and savor the top of the mountain, I fell hard. Because of paths I had taken, decisions I had made, I let go of my job, my profession, my community. I was hurting the ones I loved most deeply. And although it is difficult for me to understand now, I was following a path that I truly believed would be the best, not for me, but for everyone around me. Much in the way, I assume, that someone who ends their life can truly believe they are doing what is best for those they love the most. And there was no longer the opportunity to be productive, to accomplish anything at all, other than merely survive. I was empty, and this time was very different from the emptiness of exhaustion and being over-productive. This was the emptiness of regret and shame. But a gift materialized during this time: sacred space. And finding God in the gap.

Finding God in the Gap

I had always craved space to cultivate my spiritual wellbeing. In the busyness of my life, however, it often felt impossible to find the physical, mental and emotional space to settle into a practice. It may take complete upheaval in one's life – loss, grief, isolation – to find that space, but the emptying may be a necessary part of finding wholeness. Emptying. Kenosis in theological terms. Katabasis in epic terms. As clergy and as a Latin teacher, I've written about and taught about them both. But to experience it is something entirely different. For me, it is the meaning of resurrection. Resurrection not as a living body rising from a dead body, but rather of new life from complete emptiness. Is it possible to come to this newness, this resurrection, without the complete shattering of our lives? Yes, absolutely. But I think the secret lies in knowing our limits and keeping our productivity in check.

Whether our productivity is checked for us or we are aware enough to notice the need ourselves, we can certainly find a release from productivity in simple ways.

A daily practice of walking in the beauty of creation, listening for the chirps of birds, or watching the colors change in the trees.

But the rain is falling sideways, and the wind is just too gusty for a long walk.

Or the practice of yoga and the cherished moments of *shavasana*.

But there are four people going in different directions in the house, all needing different things. Or reading scripture or poetry or creating lyrics for a new song.

But the words evoke the loss experienced. And tears and grief supplant the moment set aside for daily spiritual practice.

The practice that was meant to bring grounding to our day can become another entry on our to-do list. Finding physical and mental space for a contemplative practice is a challenge. In that challenge, however, lies the gift of the gap.

Eckhart Tolle in his book *A New Earth: Awakening Your Life's Purpose*,[13] reaches out to those who are seeking stability through spiritual practice. 'Discover inner space by creating gaps in the stream of thinking.' Tolle leads us through the discovery of stillness. 'Stillness is the language God speaks.' And assures us that we can find it first simply in the gap between thoughts. Between breaths. Even when we cannot see space, it is there simply in that gap between thoughts. Time and location become irrelevant.

Stop reading for a moment. You do not need to get to the end of the chapter. You do not need to think about anything. Find a gap. A pause. A breath.

Perhaps you have noticed that I often do not write in complete sentences. After decades of teaching the importance of correct sentence structure in the classroom, I have found the beauty in the gaps created when the sentences are not completed. That create pause for a simple and incomplete thought. God is in the gap.

Finding Something in Nothing

Tao Te Ching – Lao Tzu – chapter 11:

Thirty spokes share the wheel's hub;
It is the center hole that makes it useful.
Shape clay into a vessel;
It is the space within that makes it useful.
Cut doors and windows for a room;
It is the holes which make it useful.
Therefore profit comes from what is there;
Usefulness from what is not there.[14]

Dawn Weisbord, Eastern medicine practitioner, led a session of QiGong at an Alignment retreat. The theme of the retreat was Creating Space. She guided participants to connect their life energy, *qi* (chi), with the energy of the earth. And reminded us that it is in the space we create that we find our deepest connection. Quoting chapter 11 of the *Tao Te Ching*, she allowed us to feel, quite literally feel, the energy in the spaces. Moving our hands together and apart, the field of energy becomes palpable. Pulling the *qi* from the ground beneath us, the spaces between our arms and bodies wrap us in the *qi* that walks with us. Gathering the *qi* from the sky above, we are washed in a rainbow of light in the space that drapes from our head to our toes. It is in the space that the *qi* is felt. It is the space in the window that allows us to see through to the world we inhabit. It is in the cavity of the clay vessel that the divine is held. It is the spaces between the spokes of the wheel that make it turn. *Therefore profit comes from what is there. Usefulness from what is not there.* It is in the nothingness times of our life, that maybe, just maybe, we find more usefulness in our lives. A deeper connection to our life energy. Our meaning. Or the fact that we may not need meaning. We are enough.

God as a Verb in the Space Between

In the quest to define God as something other than Zeus, or anthropomorphic in any way, we often turn to abstract nouns. A power. A force. Love. Spirit. Energy. Source. I challenged a group of young people to think beyond even these abstract nouns in their attempts to define the divine. They landed on verbs. God is in helping others. In reaching out your hand to someone fallen. In hurting with someone who hurts. And then the mystery dawned on them. Perhaps God is not even the verbs, but God is in that space between two people where the verb is happening. The space between giving and receiving. The infinitesimal gap where connection is forming. It is the space between breaths. The gap between thoughts. The open space in the window, the vessel, the wheel.

So perhaps in our quest to find space, in body, mind and spirit, for our contemplative practices, we need only look for the gap. Between the raindrops and gusts of wind. In the sigh between the tears. In the pause after exhale – when we know that our lungs will fill again. God is in the gaps. In every living and breathing moment, not just when we settle into deep meditation or preordained practice. We only need to mind the gap.

Keeping Our Productivity in Check

To maintain the practice of knowing our limits, how do we keep our productivity in check in the midst of lives that are filled with deadlines and tasks to be accomplished? Amidst people who are in need of our help. When the turning of new seasons brings new challenges. Having been in the field of education for most of my life in the United States, Labor Day weekend will perhaps always mark the beginning of the new year for me. The excitement of creating welcome-back activities for students, decorating the classroom, creating spaces where all would experience belonging, shuffling through twenty different to-do lists at the same time. There was always a distinct lurch from the sabbath sensibility of summer into the pressure of productivity. I was the sprinter crouching into starting position, muscles taut, eyes locked, ready to run the September to June race that defines the academic life. But once the pistol fires, what would it look like to amble along the track? People would surely stare, wonder why I was not in it to win it. Scold or encourage to pick up the pace, join the race. Or might they pause to look back and see that I was noticing the tiny yellow flowers that line the gravel path? Might they join me in breathing in the moment? Might it be possible to keep our productivity in check and notice the path that lies ahead is lined with encounters that are crying out to be savored.

Bronwen Mayer Henry captures the essence of the slow-motion run for me in her beautiful book *Radioactive Painting: How a Cancer Treatment Lit Up My Creative Practice*,[15] where she speaks of the space that she allows herself, the space not to be the best. She 'chooses joy over perfection' – which is also her Instagram[16] handle.

She writes:

> *I'm reminded of the notion that one reason children are such good learners is that they have a higher tolerance for not being good at something. As adults we expect ourselves to be proficient out of the gate, and this expectation paralyzes us.*

Bronwen engages in the spiritual practice of painting 'big', allowing herself not to feel unworthy of the large canvases and bold strokes that bring the trees and flowers that she cherishes into new life. Space: temporal and physical. Mental and spiritual. Slowing. Noticing. Breathing. And yes, producing. But with a depth of connection and peace that feeds instead of depleting.

Tricia Hersey founded the Nap Ministry in 2016 with this powerful message, that our focus on the race of productivity is a product of our oppressive society and grind culture. She preaches that we must feel worthy of rest. That it is one of our most basic needs. That moving forward is not possible without our focus on the spaces that allow for our spiritual wellbeing. In her book *Rest Is Resistance: A Manifesto* she writes:

> *Productivity should not look like exhaustion. The concept of laziness is a tool of the oppressor. A large part of your unraveling from capitalism will include becoming less attached to the idea of productivity and more committed to the idea of rest as a portal to just be.*[17]

Even as she promotes this powerful book, she is very clear that she will not take on more engagements to speak about this work if it interferes with her own need to rest. She is a strong witness to us that she can allow her creative work the space to live and breathe on its own. And in the process she is refueled with the focus and strength to write more and to minister more effectively.

Heidi Barr in her book *Collisions of Earth and Sky: Connecting with Nature for Nourishment, Reflection, and Transformation* reminds us that our connection with the simple things and 'the ordinary actions of our days' is the fuel for moving us forward. Stopping to notice, to be in nature, to create space and time, are essential to our wellbeing.[18] The simplicity of the message itself is easy to acknowledge, but so challenging even in that simplicity. These three women write with a depth of understanding of the human experience that feels so basic. And so deeply critical. Can we shift our perspective on what productivity looks like? Can the moments spent gazing and daydreaming and napping and watching the bird fly overhead and putting paint to canvas and stopping to listen to a song without it being in the background be the most essential work we do today?

Heidi's poem *Seeking Wisdom* in her collection of poetry, *Slouching Toward Radiance*, has been a guiding point for me as I begin this season of keeping my productivity in check.

> *Give silence*
> *enough room to expand*
> *so those old temptresses of*
> *growth, productivity, and worthiness*
>
> *don't run away*
> *with your peace.*

*Seek out practice wisdom
in all its messy,*

*uncomfortable nuances.
Sometimes voices in old,
tired stories need to fade
so new chapters have room to bloom.*[19]

Practice

LOVING WORDS

There is a rich Latin word *finitimi* which means boundaries, limits. It is derived from another Latin word *finis* (end) from which we have those things that are *finite* and *infinite*, with and without end. The word is used to define the boundaries of your property. But what is found at the boundaries of your property? Your neighbors. The word *finitimi* can also be translated as *neighbors* or *neighboring*. Our Germanic word neighbor is simply someone who dwells near us. But I find something fascinating in the dual use of *finitimi* as both the limits of our own property and the neighbors that we encounter at those boundaries. In going to the very limits, there we find our neighbor. In knowing our limits, there is the opportunity to find connection to the other.

RETHINK

In limiting our drive to produce, we can find sacred space even in the gap between two thoughts.

REFRAME

In emptiness, in lack of productivity, in recognizing our limits, there is an important space of openness, of nothingness, that is, in fact, everything. Let us reframe emptiness as the sacred space where we are one with the divine.

REIMAGINE

Instead of making a *to-do* list that awaits your waking eyes in the morning, make an *I-did* list at the end of the day. Perhaps it is already your practice to journal or keep a gratitude diary. But try this. Very simply list the things you did that day, instead of what you need to do. Surprise yourself that perhaps the simplest acts of choosing joy over perfection were the most important moments of the day.

Part Two

Practice Release

Chapter 5
Ground Level

Practice humility
Not as an act of lowering
But as an expression of nearing.

Teaching at Ground Level

'I can't remember the last time I touched grass,' announced a student in my classroom out of the blue. I was giving my daily reminder to look at me instead of their computer. During pandemic school days, I tried every digital tool I could find to make language learning online more engaging. We practiced verb forms with GimKit. We worked through translations using Pear Decks. We made connections using Padlets and Jamboards – and I felt like a wizard transforming my decades of teaching tricks into digital experiences. Then I just wanted eye contact back. I worried that I had contributed to the pandemic of digital addiction. Connection via screen. And when that student proclaimed that he couldn't remember the last time he had touched grass, I felt certain that I had also contributed to their disconnection from the earth. So out we went. Verb conjugations could wait. We needed to touch the grass.

It was a rainy January day, and I must say I was hard pressed to find a patch of grass that looked even remotely touchable. Until we bent down. And put our palms into puddles from which sparse spiky blades were standing firm and green. We bounced our hands on them, letting our fingers feel their strength, as they were staying the winter. Perhaps they were not standing as close to their neighboring blades as they did in summer, and their growth was dormant, but there they were, ready to be touched. Ready to acknowledge that they had seen better days. Ready to share a million life lessons with us. We were acknowledging the earth from which we have come and to which we will return.

Back in my classroom I regrounded my teaching practices in my pre-pandemic strategies. We knelt in circles on the floor to tap the present tense of verbs in a rhythmic pattern. We spread words on torn up bits of paper all over the ground to decode the highly inflected Latin sentences, to piece together meaning from seemingly random forms. The moments on ground level were ones of connection and engagement and living practice. Our hands may not have been in the dirt or bouncing on the grass, but somehow at this level we were more connected.

The central or perhaps signature piece of my teaching years was something I called *Tempus Fabulae* – the time of the story. It appeared when students might least have expected it. In the middle of teaching something else, sometimes even in the middle of a test, I would slip the words *Tempus Fabulae* gently up on the board, and the students immediately fell into position on the floor in a circle of silence. We invoked the Musa, the goddess Calliope, with the words *Musa, mihi fabulam memora. Muse, remember the story for me* – chanted three times until the story was breathed into me, and I told an instalment of the *Odyssey* or the *Aeneid*. The telling of the episodes was dramatic, often resulting in the teacher in the classroom below me asking if the *Odyssey* was happening again. The journeys, the trials, became a part of these students. They saw allusions to the epics in their other classes and in their lives.

When students come back to visit from college and beyond, the experiences at ground level are the ones they remember the most. Particularly moving was two students in their late twenties who asked to meet with me to discuss how *Tempus Fabulae* had changed their lives. One was deciding to begin the process of ordination as a Zen Buddhist monk, and he had identified this as arising from *Tempus Fabulae*. Another was about to undergo gender-affirming surgery and said that they had found the strength to begin this journey from the lessons learned in *Tempus Fabulae*. My own decision to go to seminary surfaced during *Tempus Fabulae*. For me, the decisions that move me forward happen when I am at ground level. Lowered from anything lofty. Rooted. Grounded. In touch with the earth from which I came.

Prayer at Ground Level

My prayer practices feel more connected to the divine when I take them to the ground as well. Poet Chelan Harkin reminds me, 'Our access to divinity is as deep as our access to humility.'[20] During QiGong my feet are planted on the earth. Embodied prayer. I draw the qi/chi up from the earth and with a sweep of my hands from head to shoulders and down the length of my legs, I release it to the earth again. My whole being is infused with the exchange of energy with the earth. My meditation and yoga practice is on ground level. Joining my Hindu friends in special ceremonies – in celebration and in grieving – our feet are bare and we are gathered on the ground around sacred symbols from the earth. In the Sikh gurdwara for prayer, again I am on the ground, humbled to the earth. Into the next room for langar, sitting in rows on the floor, a community shares food with anyone who is there to be in fellowship. Worship and fellowship on ground level – I can't help but think that in this position of connection to the earth, we are more connected to one another.

The earth is our home. Our teacher. The support beneath our feet. The source of our energy. Our access to divinity.

We know that we fail on a daily basis to listen to her groans of pain under our neglect. Yet still she gives us her everything. She tells us what divinity is. That which longs to be in relationship with us. Our source and our strength, even when we turn away in neglect. Perhaps, though, by taking our prayer to ground level, we can cultivate that bond. We can turn to her divinity and accept her limitless foundation.

In the Presbyterian church in which I was raised, there are few opportunities to take knee to ground. A laying-on of hands in ordination. The taking of vows. During these pivotal moments in our journeys of faith and life, we literally humble ourselves before God. The bending of the knee is an ancient symbol of reverence before a higher power. But perhaps we could reframe that. Maybe we are taking ourselves closer to our God. Not bending ourselves in obeisance, but literally turning closer to the divine, seeking closer relationship. Taking ourselves to the root of our foundation and faith as we find God in all of creation. Those of the Reformed tradition in Christianity generally do not kneel in prayer, although John Calvin suggested that if it helps you feel a deeper connection to God, then by all means kneel.

The image of my father kneeling in prayer at the very back of the chancel is engraved in my mind. But recently, Presbyterian theologian and author Belden Lane reminded me of another way in which my father ritually took knee to ground. I had not remembered it, I think, because technically I never saw it. There was a hymn before the sermon. And halfway through the singing of the hymn, the commanding figure that was about to step into the pulpit and proclaim God's word disappeared. If you happened to look up from your hymnal at the end of the second verse, it would seem he had evaporated. But Belden was able to see the minister who was his mentor at the time from his place on the lectern side. My father took to ground before stepping into that pulpit. My father, who always had a stone from Iona in his pocket, who tapped his walking stick rhythmically on the ground as he walked the roads of his beloved homeland, my father knew that the ground beneath his feet was the place where he was in deepest connection with his creator.

By taking everything, from our practices of prayer to our interactions in work and worship, to ground level, perhaps we can re-engage our connection to earth. Come into right relationship with the divine. May our eyes soar to the skies. May we breathe the air that fuels our lungs. But may our feet be firmly planted and our hearts rooted in the earth which gives us life.

When Circumstances Don't Allow

There are times, however, when circumstances do not allow us to lower ourselves to ground level. When our knees do not bend, when we cannot even find a patch of unpaved ground, still she is there. How beautiful to recognize that the earth is ever-present beneath us, nonetheless. Below the three levels of the apartment building. Under the foundation of the marble floor of the cathedral. Beneath the hospital bed and all the layers of piping and cement. She is there. Even flying in a metal container thousands of miles above her surface, we are still held by her pull. It is not necessary to touch soil to know that seeds are lying dormant within it, to sprout when the time comes.

But why do we limit ourselves just to Mother Earth? She herself is part of a vastness quite beyond comprehension. She herself held in place by an even greater pull. Part of the eternal vibration. The Om that echoes from a timeless and limitless infinite. But we are here and we are now. And our connection is to the earth beneath our feet.

When I come back to Iona, I feel a particularly strong pull to the earth. The fact that it is known to be a 'thin place' notwithstanding, there is something that feels differently aligned in my body and my breath when I am here. And I think it has something to do with indigeneity. I was born in the United States. I was raised there. Educated there. Raised my children there. It is home. Every summer, however, we traveled back to our family that lived in Scotland and made the pilgrimage to Iona. It is the place where my father found his call to work for justice through ministry. It is the place where my son dropped to one knee and proposed to the woman he loves with all his heart. It is a place of sanctuary and of challenge. Of respite and of hard work. Of whipping winds and brilliant sunshine. Of wilderness and community. And here I feel at home.

One day I was making the trek to the south side of the island to the spot where Columba, having left Ireland, was said to have landed his coracle. Stepping foot on the island to which he brought Christianity while honoring the Celtic traditions indigenous to the land with its respect for the rhythms and rituals of the earth. As I crested the hill that brings into view Columba's Bay, a powerful surge of energy lifted my hands from my side. Not a gust of wind, but the earth's life force buoying my fingers, hands, elbows, shoulders. I had never felt anything so palpable. I received her push against my arms and returned it with equal force. The earth and I were one. Had I feathers, this exchange of energy would have lifted me, soaring to the bay and swooping around the labyrinth embedded in the grass beyond the stony beach.

'We are all indigenous to some place,' teaches Indigenous author Randy Woodley in his book *Becoming Rooted*.[21] He urges us to be aware of the reality that embedded deep within our own DNA, even as an amalgamation of different ethnicities, we have each originated from a particular place or places on this Earth. We are rooted in very physical ways by our indigeneity. But what happens when we are displaced or our land is colonized? 'Planting your roots on the land in which you live is the only way to restore harmony and balance on Earth.' Randy lives by the indigenous wisdom that the earth is beneath us no matter what. Even when we cannot physically touch it. Even if we do not live in a place that is native to us. So we stay present in the place where we are. We honor the needs of the place where we are. We create community in the place where we are. And then we are home.

I feel very fortunate to be able to travel to the place with which my DNA feels aligned. I know that I damage the Earth in the ways that I need to travel to this place, and I live by the Iona Community's commitment of accountability for how I use my resources in other areas of my living. But it is not home. Where I was born is home. Where I gave birth to my children is home.

This morning before I sat to write this chapter, I climbed the hill on Iona, Dun I. I wanted to take the energy from the earth into my being before I put words on the paper. I wanted to take myself to ground level. My version of my father's prayer before preaching perhaps. When I reached the top, the wind was so strong that I could not stand upright. The rain started to pour. So I touched the cairn and quickly started my descent. And as it was, I could not make my way back down without touching each clump of wild grass, each slippery stone, each trickling lick of rainfall cutting new paths between the pebbles. Each touch secured my step and guided my descent. She held me and whispered to me to carry on. That even when I had found the shelter of a dry room to put my thoughts into words, she would still be there as my support. I sit here on the floor of my room on Iona that has no windows, no desk, no seeming connection to the earth and realize that it is my posture that matters. I needed to be on ground level whether my fingers were touching soil or not. It is the posture of releasing myself to connection, to humility, to oneness with the divine.

Practice

LOVING WORDS

Humility – lowering ourselves to the *humus*, the earth. Humility carries all sorts of connotations of lowering oneself before a higher power, of maintaining a lesser position with grace, of passivity, which are all a whisper away from images of oppression and subjugation. But the *humus* from which come our *humble* stances of *humility* is the very substance that makes us *human*. It is not the *terra*, the lands which can be possessed and divided. It is not the *solum* which is simply the lowest part or base of that on which we build. It is the stuff that we can dig our fingers into, from which the seeds sprout, that nourishes and nurtures us. By taking a stance of humility, we are connecting ourselves to creation, to the mystery and wonder of life that is both beyond our comprehension and the most tangible part of what we are.

RETHINK

Prayer and practice at ground level can open us to a deeper feeling of connection: with the earth, with one another, and with the divine.

REFRAME

If the posture of kneeling carries the image of obeisance, reframe this as one of creating connection with the earth.

REIMAGINE

As my homiletics professor, Karyn Wiseman, taught us, get out of the damn pulpit. She had a strong dislike for the position of ministers above the congregation, separated by layers of space and learning. I was never fond of the wandering preacher practice, the chat and stroll style of informality in proclaiming the word of God, but could a preacher share wisdom with circles gathered on the floor? As it is at the gurdwara where all take to the floor for the readings from the Guru Granth Sahib, the sacred Sikhi songs and writings.

Earth Teach Me

Jennifer Folayan served as a Cultural Specialist at the Healing Lodge of Seven Nations in Spokane, Washington. Her connection to the earth is always present in prayer. She shared this Ute prayer with Alignment in the sanctuary of trees.

Earth teach me quiet ~ as the grasses are still with new light.
Earth teach me suffering ~ as old stones suffer with memory.
Earth teach me humility ~ as blossoms are humble with beginning.
Earth teach me caring ~ as mothers nurture their young.
Earth teach me courage ~ as the tree that stands alone.
Earth teach me limitation ~ as the ant that crawls on the ground.
Earth teach me freedom ~ as the eagle that soars in the sky.
Earth teach me acceptance ~ as the leaves that die each fall.
Earth teach me renewal ~ as the seed that rises in the spring.
Earth teach me to forget myself ~ as melted snow forgets its life.
Earth teach me to remember kindness ~ as dry fields weep with rain.
An Ute Prayer

Chapter 6
Contemplation in Community

Practice together
Dance and sing, laugh and cry,
Share stories and supper.
Contemplation in community.

Contemplation Does Not Have to be Done Alone

This year we lost a giant, the spiritual teacher and writer Rev. Dr. Barbara A. Holmes, whose work was focused on African-American spirituality and mysticism. Her pivotal book *Crisis Contemplation: Healing the Wounded Village* advances the understanding that contemplative practice does not only heal at the individual level, but also in the face of crises that affect communities: 'Natural disaster, pandemics, violent oppression, systemic dehumanization, othering, and microaggressions that destroy health and wellbeing.'[22] She breaks open the idea of contemplation – inviting joy and movement into the practices that bring wellbeing and wholeness and connection where there is brokenness.

Perhaps the most common understanding of the contemplative life is that it is one of solitude and silence. We think of the desert fathers leading lives of ascetic monasticism as hermits, the bleak desert terrain becoming one in our mind with contemplation. We picture the Buddhist practice of stillness and silence, connecting with divine presence through turning inward. Dr. Holmes, however, introduces crisis contemplation as the opening of a portal to the inner sanctum of a community that has been shattered by crisis. A response to an event or series of events that shifts the community understanding of reality. It is a falling into the center of both personal and collective being. Both. The healing practice exists in the sacred space of community, of which the individual is part.

It is here that I revert to my persistent practice as a Latin teacher of picking apart words. Contemplation. The state of being together with (*con*) the sacred space (*templum*). Contemplation involves creating sacred space, space set apart. It includes the physical space set apart, the temporal space – time – set apart, and the ritual, the action, set apart from our ordinary space. And here is where stillness enters. In order to find that contemplative space, to set it apart, we still all else. We still the chatter. We set it aside. And yes, that might include physical stillness, but let us not confuse contemplative practice with having a still body. Dr. Holmes describes the wounded village that heals in the contemplative ritual of song, and movement, and moaning, and dancing, and eating. Her beautiful expression is that 'stillness is a state of wholeness, an antidote to the fragmentation of BIPOC* people that comes with marginalization.'[23]

Interfaith Alignment was founded with the understanding that the contemplative life is nurtured in community. The creation of a community of understanding among people who seek spiritual meaning in their lives. Islam, Christianity, Judaism, Buddhism, Hinduism, Sikhism, Baha'i, Zoroastrianism, Native American and Wiccan are among the traditions represented – both in practices and in participants. Practices range from chanted sessions of prayer to expressive reflection through art. Each week people gather from their own spaces around the globe seeking connection. Connection to the divine that is within us, beyond us, and beside us. Some people come online every week, and some only attend when it is a practice that is of particular interest. Some people keep their cameras on and we recognize faces, and some never show themselves on camera. Some add comments to the chat in response to reflective prompts, and some do not ever interact. Nevertheless, they are there in community. Alignment exists because the contemplative life does not have to be the solitary life.

With the building of community comes the need for release. A release of expectations, a release of ego, and sometimes a release of what has been central to our way of operating.

---

* BIPOC = Black, Indigenous, People of Color

Building a Community of Hope

Nothing feels quite as awkward as entering the house of faith of another tradition and not understanding what to do. Are you supposed to stand now? Or kneel? When you can't follow the transliteration of the prayers fast enough to keep up, it's uncomfortable. I think it is one of the things that keeps us out of the houses of worship of other traditions. We just don't know what to expect, and we don't want to stand out for not knowing what to do. But what if we could overcome that awkwardness? Focus on being together. Reach over to someone who doesn't know what page of the prayer book we're on. Might we be able to build a stronger community of hope, if we could embrace one another's ways of being? Ways of praying? Ways of hurting and healing? Ways of pointing forward in the midst of feeling lost, forgotten and marginalized?

Barack Obama in his book *The Audacity of Hope* recognizes that the key to moving forward as a society is in seeing the other, in their struggles and in their dreams.

> *'I believe a stronger sense of empathy would tilt the balance of our current politics in favor of those people who are struggling in this society. After all if they are like us, then their struggles are our own. If we fail to help, we diminish ourselves.'*[24]

Empathy – suffering together. Feeling one another's pain. The hope for all of us lies in our ability to embrace one another. And we can't do that simply by reading the headlines. Or sending a donation to an organization that needs our support. Empathy comes from embracing the other. Sitting at table together. Singing together. Praying together, even in languages we don't understand. It is the message in the Zulu greeting *Sawubona*. 'I see you, you are important to me, and I value you.' If we can see one another, we will not be diminished. It is an act of reciprocity. It is not about one person helping another whom we have deemed of greater need. But in seeing one another, valuing and embracing one another. In this lies our hope.

And in this lies the need to let go of the assumption that our way is the only way.

When Prayer Becomes an Act of Service

I worked in a Quaker school that strove on a weekly basis to connect the school community to the testimony of service. To answer the Rev. Dr. Martin Luther King, Jr.'s 'most persistent and urgent question'

'What are you doing for others?'

A chunk of each week is set aside for students and staff to 'be of service' in the community, on and off campus. We used to steer students away from saying that they 'do service' because it makes them feel good. We tried to make them aware that the act of service is not about feeling good about ourselves for what we did for someone else. But I've changed my mind on that. It *is* about feeling good. It's about feeling good because we have stepped beyond our fear of meeting someone who in some ways might be different from us. It's about feeling good in relationship with someone else. It is about being together, seeing one another. Letting someone know they are important to us. That we value them. It *should* be about feeling good.

After decades and decades of traveling to Iona on pilgrimage, I finally had the time to be of service to this beloved community. I applied to be a volunteer for three months. I do not think I have ever, with so many others, worked so hard for the purpose of pursuing 'justice and peace in and through community'.[25] And it demanded the release of a lot, as being in community does. But as I examined what I had to let go of in order to live in community, they were all things that kept me siloed. The luxury of my own space to live, my own bathroom, cooking the food that I am used to, making my own schedule, feeling competent at my daily duties. As I struggled in the first weeks to get a grip on my new tasks, from cleaning toilets and making beds, to learning how to issue a refund on the Welcome Centre till, even knowing the correct way to refill the boxes of chocolate (i.e. not the way I was doing it), my line manager made clear that more important than any task was the interaction with people on a personal level, the sharing of stories with pilgrims who had traveled the world to visit this holy place. I so easily got caught up in wanting to be good at my new tasks that I forgot the most basic tenet of my life's practice – that I truly needed to engage to be of service. To see the other. To find stillness in the community that was ever-changing, ever cycling through new faces and new moments of sharing. The stillness of contemplation found in community comes, as Dr. Holmes teaches us, as a state of wholeness. When we are one with the sacred space of finding belonging with one another. And this type of prayer can be in song or dance, over a cup of tea and an oatcake, in the time taken to sit with a new friend to share a little bit of what makes you who you are, or in the release of needing to have things the way you like them. Just when you think that prayer might not be a part of your life, consider a time when you let go of what you needed to do and let someone change your perspective. The stillness that washed in was prayer.

Practice

LOVING WORDS

A little more about the fascinating word contemplation. Many stop at its Latin root *contemplatio*, the act of gazing at or observing closely. It is easy to see this leading to the generally accepted understanding of contemplation as an act of silence, solitude and stillness. To think of a contemplative as one engaged in deep listening and prayer. But when an English word comes so directly from a Latin word, it is always more enlightening to dig into the Latin word itself. This is what carries us to its component parts of being one (*con*) with the temple (*templum*). Once we step into the space of the temple, it does not seem so solitary anymore. We are in a place where others have come together, out of a sense of duty perhaps, or very likely seeking community and connection with their god or with their neighbors. It's interesting to remember that the Greco-Roman *templa* were not places to go in, but places to go to. And before the structures whose columns we can name from our art classes, the temples were simply open spaces, in the open air or on the land, set aside for ritual or the reading of omens. Spaces set apart. Sacred and ordinary. And, above all, connected to creation. The birds that brought signs. The winds that whispered messages. The sun that embodied divinity.

But we do not have to stop at the breaking apart of the Latin word. We can uncover another layer of soil to find the Proto-Indo-European root **tem-* which carries the meaning of cutting or dividing. It gives rise to the *templum*, the space set apart. And to other words that have to do with cutting such as *tome*, a book that might be the division of a larger work, and *anatomy*, the dividing up of the body into sections.

But it is also related to words of time such as the previously discussed *Tempus Fabulae* and the words *temporary* or *time* itself. So time and space set apart. And coming together in community. This is at the heart of contemplation.

RETHINK

Contemplation is not necessarily an act of solitude, silence and stillness.

REFRAME

We can expand the practice of contemplation by embracing the importance of community in our practice.

REIMAGINE

Time spent over a cup of tea with a friend, listening to what is on her heart, sharing what is on yours, a moment set apart, a deep listening, being seen and known – imagine this as your open temple and your prayer lifted into the gift of communion with one another.

Chapter 7
Letting Go of Labels

Practice releasing ego
The need for your way
To be the way

Shaped by Language

The way in which language shapes our thoughts and beliefs fascinates me. Tremendous power lies in the words of our sacred texts, prayers, hymns and confessions which describe God; power that defines how we are in relationship with the divine in our lives. Hence my grand plans as a church youth director of encouraging the children to examine their use of language to describe God. When we pulled ourselves away from patriarchal descriptors, and then stepped away from the notion of God being a person, or perhaps even a noun, we created a video based on our wonderings – of people being in relationship in different ways – and made the focus of our cinematic production the idea that God might not be an anthropomorphic entity or even a power, but could in fact be the label we put on instances of unconditional, supportive, loving, respectful and nurturing relationship. We played our video during our Youth Sunday morning worship service led by the children. During the service I asked the adult members of the congregation to raise their hands if they had ever in their lives turned away from their faith, doubted the existence of what we call God, left the church because they could not understand the point. I remember seeing nothing but a sea of hands and then the shocked faces of the children who were amazed that all the adults in their church family had admitted to this. Defining what God is seems so central and necessary to our lives of faith, and also so impossible. How many of these people may have turned away from their faith because the language and the labels used were inadequate for them, or even deterrent?

I left that internship to complete my studies in seminary, but the pastor called me back to be there for the children on the Sunday after the 2016 election. He wanted there to be a stable and familiar presence there for them as they dealt with the shock of their parents on that post-election day. I walked into the Sunday School room, having been away for only five months, and they were reading a passage from Genesis for their lesson. 'How do we know what God looks like,' asked one of the eight-year-old children. 'He looks like us; we were created in his image,' replied one of the older children. Argh. God had slipped back into that easily definable male image again. It was so deeply rooted in their family traditions and the words they were hearing in worship that they could not get away from the language that was shaping their experience of God.

Growing up, I too was one of those children. I had an almost vitriolic response to people who attempted to change the words of prayers and hymns to more inclusive language. I was deeply steeped even then in the importance of language and hated to think of the familiar words being altered. It felt wrong. God was our father, and we were created in his image. My father, with all his progressive interfaith sensibility, was firmly set in his very traditional use of language. I was not planning on messing with that. The greatest gift he passed on to me in relation to my faith, however, was that I should constantly question it, explore it, and poke at it. I should read and listen and be in dialogue with people of different traditions in order to challenge and broaden my understanding. As a child I eavesdropped on my father's conversations with monks and rabbis, not to hear what they were saying – I couldn't understand their discussions – but I listened to the way they questioned one another and respected one another, and I listened to the passion in those conversations. They wanted to share stories and learn from each other. They wanted just to be in communion with one another.

My father died when I was twenty. The image that remains most vivid in my mind is of him sitting under a dogwood tree in our backyard on a lawn chair, the vinyl straps sagging beneath him, a kippah on his head, a concrete Buddha under the bush in front of him, working on a sermon or writing a poem, stopping to note that a cardinal is singing in the tree. He leans over to me and says, 'We are blessed to live here.' I was unsure of what it meant to be blessed. I am still wary of using that term. But today it means to me that God was in that space. I think he knew in that space that God did not need to be defined by religion or tradition. God was the sharing of that moment. The Buddhist, Jewish and Christian traditions that had shaped his life were present in that space. His love of writing and challenging the beliefs of others was present in the work he did in that space. His love of family was in that space. The beauty of creation was in that space. He framed the divine by that space. And he let go of that traditional worship language in that space. Along with the deep love of words that he taught me, he also taught me the importance of letting them go.

In the Reformed tradition in which I was raised, there is a guiding call to be constantly aware of the present circumstances. *Ecclesia reformata semper reformanda est*: the church having been reformed, reshaped, must always be reforming. In the Presbyterian Church (USA) the constitutional documents include a Book of Order and a Book of Confessions, both of which are reissued regularly as they are amended. Most moving to me is the inclusion of twelve confessional statements that speak to one another across the centuries and across the globe in response to the needs of the time. If the circumstances arise in which the Church needs to state anew what it believes, to realign with the needs of the world, a new confession is written and/or adopted. New language and new labels. At my ordination examination I was asked the stale question put to all candidates in the presbytery. Which is your favorite confession? I rejected the question. The point of the Book of Confessions, to my understanding, was that the statements are all in conversation with one another, across the difference in language and time, across the circumstances of each generation, that we might be in community with the cloud of witnesses. Knowing the question was coming, I had carefully crafted an answer that put lines from each confession into that conversation with one another.

Alas, they still ask candidates the same question. Alas, I no longer hold my ordination. But may the reforming church be so bold as to entertain the conversation not only across confessional statements, but across traditions.

Missing the Meaning

I have a problem reading books. I love to read; good historical fiction is my favorite. But my problem is that I can't remember what a book is about after I've finished with it. It has been this way for as long as I can remember. What I can recall, however, is my emotional response to it. Many a time I have said to someone, 'You'll love this book!' I can pinpoint exactly what my feelings were, but if you want any description of the plot or setting, you're out of luck. This is why I would be a terrible member of a book club.

It is even more so with poetry. I love to listen to it being spoken. My parents and grandmother were always reciting poetry, from Robert Burns to Wordsworth. My father could do a full two hours of Shakespeare in one sitting, from memory. And even more with poetry I find the emotions that it evokes are what cling to me, not the meaning. Funny to think about how much I love words and wordplay and translations, that in the end it really isn't about the words, but about what is left when the words are gone.

I had the same problem with a conversation that just might have been one of the most important of my life – and I can't remember what was said. I have wracked my brain for years trying to recreate it, but what I do remember is that it gave me answers I needed. I remember how it made me feel.

It was a conversation I had with my father when I must have been about ten. In Sunday School the teacher had us memorize John 3:16, *for God so loved the world that he gave his only begotten son, that whosoever believed in him would have eternal life.* We left it there. No explanation needed, just memorize it. But always one to do a little bit more than expected, I carried on. The next bit was the real kicker for me. *Those who believe in him are not condemned; but those who do not believe are condemned already, because they have not believed in the name of the only Son of God.* My best friend, Liz Cohen, was going to perish. I went to my dad, distraught. This must have been my first theological conversation with my father – who died less than a decade later. And I can't remember what he said.

I have tried to recreate the conversation to the point that I think I have reinvented it, what he must have said. As I figured out and deepened my own understanding over the years, I know I have put words into his mouth in the memory of that conversation. But then it hit me, not too long ago, that it doesn't matter what he said. It matters that he gave me an understanding of God's love that was so deep, so wide, so all-encompassing that there was no possible way that God's word could ever be interpreted that my best friend was going to perish because she did not believe that Jesus Christ was the son of God. It was not the words, it was the creation of an understanding of God's love and the safety and security of being held in that love and walking forward in my love and my relationship with my friend of another faith tradition.

Words are messy. Words that shape what you believe are even messier. Theologians spend their lives untwisting and untangling words that have been passed down to us across generations and across cultures and across contexts so that they can get to the heart of what it is we believe. And so that God's word can have meaning for us right now, right here. And I have to say, I do enjoy getting caught in that tangle, but in the end there is always an overwhelming awareness that when the words are gone, we are left with a feeling that transcends words.

Interconnected and Interdependent

What would happen if we could look beyond the language and labels that shape the way we pray? If we could focus on the way our practices make us feel. On the way they shape us to live our lives.

Alignment collaborates with the Iona Community and with the Week of Prayer for World Peace committee to offer the opportunity to pray for peace with leaders from different traditions from around the world. The collaboration was initiated by a comment from the Iona Abbey Warden, Caro Penney, who noted that the written prayers prepared for this interfaith week usually had the disclaimer 'adapted from a Jewish prayer' or 'adapted from a Muslim prayer'. Why were we adapting prayers, she wondered. Why are we not using prayers from those traditions? When I remarked that this is what Alignment already offers, the spark was lit. We spent seven months building a digital platform and inviting leaders from different traditions into the conversations. We gathered video recordings of messages, chants, dances, songs, poems – all prayers for peace that were offered, one opening each day, so that whoever was praying for peace that day was praying in the practice of one particular tradition.

Beautiful, but one problem. It was only eight days. Eight traditions. What about those who were not included? On the first day, I had three separate emails asking why Bahá'í prayers were not included in the offerings. It is a horrible thing not to be included, when we do not hear our own tradition uplifted. The interesting thing here is that the Bahá'í offering was on Day 2. It was not excluded. The reaction must have come from years of experience of exclusion. It was anticipatory disappointment. But still there were only eight. Countless other traditions had not been uplifted in this project, and it was not enough to say that there would be eight other traditions represented the following year. So we built a wall. A digital prayer wall for peace. And it was populated by people around the world from a multitude of traditions, posting their prayers in images and songs and poems and single words and formal prayers in various languages, so that in itself it presented a tapestry of symbols, characters, letters, lines, colors and beauty.

Rev. Qalvy Grainsvolt, a Shinnyo-en Buddhist monk, posted a message for the Week of Prayer for World Peace, a reminder that we are called to find our interdependence. Unique traditions upheld, not melted into one voice or one way of thinking, or one intention in prayer, but interconnected. Interdependent. Certainly this, at its core, is the meaning of family. Whether we are bound by blood or ceremony, by tradition or by choice, a family is a grouping of individuals, each with their own needs and distinctive voices. Families can be a place of shelter and nurture or of hurt and harm. The ties that bind can be like a frayed rope, threads snapping or severed. And so it is in war. The household of the world, the *oikoumene*, disconnected. Rev. Qalvy urged us to pray for families caught in conflict, whether at the level of the individual, the nation or the entirety of the Earth. He offered mantras: the GOREIJU (mantra of benevolence and liberation), and one of the core chants in the Shinnyo tradition, the

Letting Go of Labels 87

JOJUAN, which is composed of two words, *Namu Shinnyo*. These words call us to be in oneness with the ever-present nature of awakening and the embodiment of inner goodness.

As we, a global community of people from widely varying traditions, prayed with Rev. Qalvy for families in conflict, our hearts and minds turned immediately to civilians caught in the ongoing humanitarian crises of war. Those waking to turn to prayer and ripped from their homes, those seeking shelter when their homes are no longer safe. Those for whom the safety of the embrace of family is ruptured. And also those who are not civilians, who are fighting for the protection of their families, homelands and heritage. For the families that have to let them go. Caught in conflict. He referenced the leader of the Shinnyo-en Buddhist order, Her Holiness Keishu Shinso Ito, who teaches that the very earth is permeated by lovingkindness, wisdom and compassion. To pray for families caught in conflict is to awaken to reconnection with all beings of the Earth.

Dr. Nirinjan Kaur Khalsa-Baker offered a prayer from the Sikh tradition which originated in 16th-century South Asia during a time of invasion, forced conversion, oppression and injustice. Dr. Nirinjan introduced the work of the Sikh gurus who were mystics, poets, musicians and warriors and who taught of the same interconnectedness of all life that Rev. Qalvy discussed. She highlighted the Sikh teachings that the dualities of grief and joy, love and hate, enemy and friend, self and other are all deceptions of our ego, our self-centered nature, *haumai*, that sees me as separate from you. And us as better than them.

Dr. Nirinjan introduced Guru Arjan's prayer sung in raag kanara, a twelve-beat rhythmic cycle, played on the Jori-Pakhawaj and sung by her mother Nirvair Kaur.

> *Bisar gaī sabh ṭāṭ parāī jab ṭe sādhsangaṭ mohi pāī. Nā ko bairī nahī bigānā sagal sang ham kao ban āī. Jo prabh kīno so bhal mānio eh sumaṭ sādhū ṭe pāī. Sabh meh rav rahiā prabh ekai pekh pekh Nānak bigsāī.*

I have totally forgotten envy of others, since blessed with the company of the awakened.
No one an enemy, and no one a stranger. We are all interconnected.
What the Divine does, I accept as good.

*This is the sublime wisdom I have received from the sages.
The One pervades all. Everywhere I look I see the One, Oh bloom in bliss!*
(Guru Granth Sahib, 1299, Guru Arjan Ji. Translated by Nirinjan Kaur Khalsa-Baker)

Dr. Khalsa describes how this song, Sukhmani Sahib, is a prayer of peace that teaches how we may cultivate a peaceful mind by replacing self-centered thought, speech and action with love for all. By meditating on the Divine Unity of Creation, pain and sorrow depart and peace dwells in our heart and mind. We perform good deeds and selflessly serve others because we see no separation and recognize the Divine Light that shines within all – enemies and friends alike.

Dr. Khalsa works closely with her Sikh sister, Valarie Kaur, whose book *Sage Warrior* explains the Sikh path of the *sant sipahi*, the sage warriors who surrendered their ego-centered nature and awakened to the responsibility to serve One and Other. To stand against injustice and defend those in need. To stand for love, justice, freedom, and equality of all, regardless of caste, class, creed, religion, social standing, sexuality, and gender identity. The first word of the Guru Granth Sahib, the sacred scripture of Sikhism, is Ik Onkar, Oneness, ever-unfolding. It represents the oneness of the Divine, the cosmos, and all of humanity. Valarie tells the story of Guru Nanak, the founder and first teacher of the Sikh tradition, who taught us to see all humanity as kin, and that separateness is an illusion. 'Ik Onkar' is the heart of Sikh wisdom and placed in gurdwaras (houses of faith) to remind all of the truth of our Oneness.

ik onkar satnam karta purakh nirbhao nirvair akaal murat ajooni saibhang gurprasaad

*Oneness, ever-unfolding
True by Name
Ever-creating
Without fear
Without hate
Timeless in form*

> *Beyond birth and death*
> *Complete within*
> *Received as*
> *Sweet divine blessing*
> (Guru Granth Sahib, ang 1, Jap, Guru Nanak Ji. Translated by Valarie Kaur and Nirinjan Kaur Khalsa-Baker)

In the beginning of my journey of faith, I think my understanding of God was of a being that was separate from me. Maybe even up there, looking down on me, protecting me, loving me. But as I have continued on my journey and embraced the beauty of other traditions into my own understanding, I now feel deeply that God is a part of my own being, as close as every breath I take. That God is present in the ache in my chest when I am in despair, the squeezing in my throat when I am anxious, the thumping in my heart when I rejoice, and the laughter that I share with friends. That I am, in fact, humanity that is one with divinity.

And being this closely connected, divinity and humanity as one,
How can we help but love ourselves because we are made of God?
How can we help but love one another, because all are made of God?
How can we help but work for the dignity and safety of all people because in this way we honor the oneness of all that is.
Ik Onkar.

Those gathered online to begin the walk through this international and interfaith week of prayer were deeply moved by the open sharing of prayers and poems chanted by Haleh Liza Gafori with her new and bold translations of the work of 13th-century Sufi poet Rumi. One theme highlighted was the way in which we can open our hearts to love and peace through the power and joy of awe. Haleh captures the beauty of the words that invite us to dissolve ego, to walk in the humility of a humanity that shares one spirit, even amidst the devastation of war. As we watched the horrors of war unfold, Haleh called us to continue to pray for peace – for what else can we do?

On that first day of the Week of Prayer for World Peace, the door on the digital prayer platform opened to a Jewish prayer that called on us not to let fear overwhelm us. And the day closed with Muslim prayers inviting us into the space where the waters of humanity flow as one body. May even the simple experience of praying *with*, not just *for*, people of other traditions call us to the walk of peace.

> '*Shatter the jug, the water is one.*'
> Rumi, translated by Haleh Liza Gafori[26]

Practice

LOVING WORDS

In my work with Alignment, where we offer resources and sessions of prayer and meditation, of wisdom and wonderings, from many different traditions, I use the word *tradition* instead of religion or faith. I also use different words to express some understanding of the divine within us, beside us and beyond us. Not all traditions would consider themselves to be a religion or a faith. And not all traditions would name a divine being. Not all traditions are comfortable with the use of pronouns when talking about God or even capturing in words what is most sacred in their hearts. The word tradition references that which has been passed to us by those who have walked this way before us. *Tradere* = to hand over. We hold in our hands something to be shaped to our own understanding and our own experience, to our own needs and visions. Just as we come from a place of origin and may feel splintered from it, so in our spiritual traditions, in the roots of our faith, we may find places where we feel in conflict. The importance of the word tradition lies in that image of something that has been handed over to us, that warms in the shape of our cupped hands.

RETHINK

The language used in our traditions shapes our understanding.

REFRAME

My understanding, my faith, is strengthened when in communication with other traditions. My prayers feel more deeply connected when they are connected to those of other traditions. For me, when prayer doesn't work, I now know that my understanding of prayer has been too limited. My expectations too narrow.

REIMAGINE

What if all prayers could be lifted, all voices honored, all beings interconnected and interdependent, all languages used and no languages needed? What if we understood everything to be an act of prayer?

Chapter 8
What We Let Go and What We Carry Forward

Practice
Leaving behind
And looking forward

Threshold Moments

The ritual of departure was painful, but each step was carefully choreographed. After my father spent his seminary years and early ministry working with George MacLeod on the rebuilding of Iona Abbey, he and my mother emigrated to the United States. It was not something that they wanted to do, but the call to work for justice and peace in the deep south of the United States in the 1940s was strong. When they left Scotland, they did not know how or when or if they would be able to return. My mother thought that her first encounter with mosquitoes that made her entire arm swell boded well for their need to return. She told me stories of hiding her tears from her new husband in those early days of immigration, wanting to be as supportive as she could of his work. Her twenty-one years of life to that point had not taken her past the family treks on foot into the highlands or on the bus to Glasgow. And now she was standing on the threshold of an entirely new life. New marriage, new country, new worldview. And she lived in the liminal space of looking back with longing and looking forward with hope-filled trepidation.

She became the talk of the town in Birmingham, Alabama. A young Scottish lass who was stunningly beautiful. The newspapers commented on what this young minister's wife wore to church and the luncheons she hosted for women. She lived embarrassed that the people of the city would find out that her clothes had come from thrift shops and that she had left school when she was fourteen to earn money for the family during the war. But what struck everyone that she met was the beauty that radiated from the very core of who she was. Her ability to make every single person she met feel known, seen, heard. She accomplished much by turning the phrase that we all throw away, 'How are you?', into an act of deep communication and communion by shifting the emphasis. 'How *are* you?' We teased her that she could not go into a coffee shop without carrying the life story of the waitress out with her when she left. People shared their lives with her, because she sat in the liminal space with them. Holding their pasts and gearing them ever so gently into a view of their own hope-filled future. And being present. So very present to where each and every person stood.

She and my father ministered together. He from the pulpit and she from the bedside of those who were ailing. And throughout their years together, they stood in the threshold spaces of life.

It was years before they were able to have children and to begin the yearly journey back to Scotland, to family, to the land that meant so much to them, and to Iona. This was all I knew. Summer was Scotland. There was never any thought that we might go elsewhere for the summer holidays. And there was never any plan other than that my parents would return permanently in retirement. But at the end of every summer we, as a family, re-enacted the dreadful scene of emigration.

My uncle would announce that the nights were drawing in, and a feeling of anticipatory depression moved across us all like a pall, those staying in Scotland and the four of us leaving. I would help my granny put up jars of marmalade for the winter. We would buy enough rolls of Polo mints to get us through a year of Sunday sermons. And we would pack our cases with trinkets to hang in our house in the States to remind us that we were not in Scotland. Then came the night of the final goodbyes. Every year.

Each family group came to my granny's house for their turn to say goodbye. Granny busied herself in the kitchen making round after round of cups of tea and biscuits. Keeping a brave face on. Then we took to the threshold of the front door for the long wave goodbye. I was glad when the aunts and uncles left in a car because walking only prolonged the final wave from the doorstep. Peering over the hedge for one last wave till they were out of sight. Then the next group of cousins came, and back to the threshold.

> The morning comes and the smell of dark air is suffocating
> No time for fresh rolls this morning
> Just bread and marmalade and a little cheese grilled for strength
> The bags placed at the door last night are shuffled into the car
> Before the rounds are made
> To every house where everyone who already said goodbye last night
> Was waiting at their own doorstep now for a final wave
> Unless of course they were coming with us to the airport
> Where those waves would linger all the way down the corridor
> onto the plane
> Diesel fumes preparing my lungs for a different type of air to breathe
> The smell of our house, unoccupied for months, awaiting our return.

We were actors in a play called Emigration. Not forced out of our homes by famine or war. Not going to a place unknown. We would be back again next year to play out the exact scenes once more. But this routine made me critically aware that life is lived in a series of threshold moments. Although we never did let go of this family trauma, I believe it made my parents' ministry as deeply connected as it was. They held everyone they met in that liminal space of honoring their past, pointing them bravely forward, but most important of all, standing closely with them in the inbetween.

Liminal Spaces Looking Back and Forward

Liminal spaces and times (Latin *limen* = threshold) are those opportunities that have reflection deeply rooted at their core. Reflection, the word so aptly partnered with meditation and contemplative practice, is literally a turning back. A variation on the theme of introspection, looking within. Every one of these words is steeped in Latin roots that elevate the practices of taking time to stop, take stock, ponder. With liminal spaces, however, and thresholds and the Roman god Janus himself, there is more than one direction. We are prompted not just to turn back or turn inward, but to look ahead. We turn back but we look intentionally forward as well.

Different traditions offer us quite a number of these opportunities to stand at the threshold throughout the year. In the cooling days of autumn, the Celtic tradition offers the celebration of Samhuinn, a time when the veil between the worlds is thin.

It is the threshold
between the old year and the new year
between summer and winter
between growing/harvesting and storing/preserving
between outside and inside
between now and then
between heaven and earth
between life and death
between humanity and the spirit world
between this side of the door and the other

During Samhuinn celebrations, we look with gratitude at what has passed, but stand alert to recognize what is on the other side of the veil.

In Jewish tradition, the high holy days of Rosh Hashanah, the head of the year, and Yom Kippur, allow us to take stock of the relationships in our lives as we make amends. The intention is a renewal of what is made right. Sealed in the Book of Life for another year, we move forward, forgiven, washed clean, aware of how to live our lives until the moons bring us back to this threshold again. Traditions of atonement and prayerful days of fasting and repentance in the Islamic tradition of Ramadan and the Christian observance of Lent are also threshold times, marked by looking back and also pointing forward.

Tết, the Vietnamese celebration of the Lunar New Year, is marked by Buddhist followers of Thich Nhat Hanh in Plum Village with a time of deep reflection and mindful breathing. Even in a tradition that focuses with such awareness on the present moment, there is in this new year celebration an element of honoring the ancestors, forgiving those who have brought suffering in the past year, and stepping forward into the new year with intention and renewal. When Thay died days before *Tết*, his followers continued the tradition of offering parallel verses for the new year celebration. The parallel verses are often hung in doorways on diamond-shaped pieces of paper. In the comings and goings, as the year turns new, they are a reminder to embrace the threshold moment.

> *Sitting in freedom on this sacred land*
> *Walking in peace everywhere on earth*[27]

Brigid of Kildare, the Celtic saint who lived around 500 CE, was a great proponent of reaching beyond one's own traditional spiritual understandings. She was said to have been born in the doorway of her house to a Christian mother and Druid father, in the liminal light of early morning. John Philip Newell writes that Brigid urged us to stand with courage at the thresholds that we come upon in our lives.[28] For there is the place where we open ourselves to suffering with one another. There we find a heart of compassion. She understood that we are stronger when we open ourselves to one another's practices.

Prayer as a Liminal Space

The liminal space is a place of transition as much as it is a place of presence. It is where we take pause to look back with intention. To see what has helped us grow and what has held us back. Whom we have helped and whom we have hurt. Where we have walked and left no trace and where we have left footsteps to follow. It is where we take a deep breath to move into the hereafter. And we make the decision about what to let go of and what to carry forward. In the threshold is divine presence. And each pause with intention is a prayer.

Traditional prayers at threshold moments might ask for forgiveness for what has been, and for guidance for what is to be. But here's the tricky part: there is no reality other than the threshold itself. The prayer is standing in that moment of threshold. And being aware of the divine in the doorway with you. Loving you no matter what lies behind. Loving you no matter what lies ahead.

The image that sticks in my mind of those difficult summer farewells was all four of us, my brother, my mother, my father and I, stuffed into the narrow doorway of 6 Strathview Terrace, waving till we saw the last fingertip of a wave disappear down the road. And in my mind I know my granny was somehow in the doorway too. Although she wasn't leaving. She didn't need to wave goodbye, and she certainly would not have fit into the doorway with the four of us already squeezed in tightly. But I knew she was there too. With her brave face on. With her heart breaking. With her care for every single one of us, those staying and those leaving. She held the threshold space. And in her I knew the divine.

My parents never did make it back to Scotland to retire. My father died of a heart attack right at his age of retirement. My mother lived twenty-three more years, traveling back to Scotland every summer. On my yearly visits back now, when I go to the graveside where we buried their ashes in the village where they met, no matter how hard it is raining, the sun comes out. I walk up and down the rows of the graveyard, taking note of all the wavers from summers past. I pause to wonder what lies ahead for me in the years that remain until my children carry my ashes across the sea. And then I remember, there is no greater reality than that shining sun. They are all with me with every step I take on this good earth. We are all squeezed into this threshold moment. And Granny, she's there too.

Practice

LOVING WORDS

How do threshold days so richly rooted in spiritual traditions compare to our New Year's celebrations? The time when many make resolutions, start new practices, realign with former, healthier habits. When we approach the turning of the year in our Western, Christian-rooted calendar, the significance of the date feels weak at best. The two-faced Roman god Janus, for whom January is named, was appropriately named for the doorway (Latin: *janua*) in which he stood. Janus so aptly represented this threshold month with his faces looking back and looking ahead. Or was he looking inward and pointing himself outward? Perhaps we can attribute to him something a little more contemplative as we recognize the importance of liminal spaces in our lives.

But January wasn't even the first month of the year for the Romans using the pre-Julian calendar. March, the namesake of the god of war Mars, marked the Roman new year. In like a lion. The Romans lunged into their new year with dancing priests, the Salii, in full armor. They renewed the sacred fire of Rome. With Julius Caesar's adjustments to the calendar, and a new month to mark the beginning of the year, Janus turned out to be a rather appropriate figure for this time. And still today, with a nod and a wink to the god of thresholds, we give great significance to our New Year's Eve celebrations as a liminal moment, when in actuality there are many traditions that offer meaningful threshold celebrations throughout the year.

RETHINK

Do our prayers look back and look forward, or do they hold us in the present moment?

REFRAME

Understand the threshold not as a brief moment of transition but as the place where we hold all that we are, the pain and the joy. Holding this space with another is a powerful form of prayer.

REIMAGINE

Could there be a practice of corporate prayer that holds this type of presence for those who are congregated? In which every person present might feel held in the reality of their liminal space? In such a space, each one would feel known, and seen, and heard.

Part Three

Practice Naming

Chapter 9

Exchanging Our Exhale

Practice breathing

∼

deeply

Breath prayers

I shared a bed with my granny during those summer months spent in Scotland. It was a council house the size of the flat I now live in alone, but occupied by six of us. My mother and father had the bedroom that faced the front of the house. My brother slept on the sofa cushions laid on the floor in front of the coal fire. My uncle hoisted himself up the small hole to the attic to sleep on the unfloored rafters on a plank of wood. And my granny and I were royalty in the back bedroom with a hot water bottle shared between our ice block feet. Two peas in a pod. Two Megs in a bed. Whispering the night away with our secrets and our giggles. Until it came time to ease ourselves to sleep. 'A deep breath,' she'd say. As deep as it can be. Without ever knowing that guided breathing meditations would be part of the spiritual practice of many in decades to come, my granny said her final prayer at night as a deep breath. There were no words necessary for this most meaningful of prayers shared between us. It was a conscious moment of connection. With a surrender of the weight that she carried through the day, she knew she was resting under a blanket of divine love.

My parents, on the other hand, taught me that my night-time prayer should be a litany of names of those whom I wanted God to hold in love and light. I could see my list of prayer names in concentric circles. Mum, Dad, Bobby, Granny in the center circle. Aunts, uncles and cousins in the next circle of prayer. Then friends, from school, from church, from the neighborhood. Then the circles became defined by areas of need. Those who were sick. Those who did not have enough food or a home. There were no names in those outer circles of prayer. Sometimes I imagined them, thinking my prayer would be more effective if I named the nameless.

But summer brought respite from the naming practice of prayer. 'Breathe deeply,' she'd say. They were all held in those breaths. Every name, not uttered, but breathed. My granny taught me that prayer was connected to my wellbeing. It was not about lifting the names aloud with measured intention. It was about taking the names into my heart, into my lungs, through my breath and allowing them to reside in that place where God also was.

Breath prayer has been a practice as long as there has been breath and as long as there has been prayer. Monks of the early centuries of Christianity used breath prayer to answer Paul's call to pray without ceasing, centering their prayers on every breath they took. Breathing is the one thing we do without ceasing. Even when we are unaware. Even when we are sleeping.

But it was a practice in many traditions before Christianity. In Hinduism the reciting of mantras is connected to the breath. *Om* is the breath of the universal vibration that is infinite in time and space. Rumi described the breath of love that can take us all the way to infinity. The reciting of the *shema* in Judaism, 'Hear O Israel, the Lord our God, the Lord is one,' and the *gathas* in Buddhism also connect prayer and meditation to the breath. Connecting prayer to our breath in every way as we move throughout our day makes us aware of life itself. As the word *spirit* is rooted in the Latin verb *spirare*, to breathe, so we speak of the divinity that is held in our every breath. In becoming aware of our breathing, we can also become aware of the spirit, present with us, one with us, as close to us as our breath.

Thich Nhat Hanh, beloved Buddhist monk who breathed his last earthly breath just a few years ago, taught about the practice of breath as mindfulness, of being in the present. That every breath can be a prayer. Brushing our teeth. Taking a step. With every step and every breath we hold our ancestors with us, present with us. 'Breathing in, I calm body and mind. Breathing out, I smile. Dwelling in the present moment I know this is the only moment.'[29] Christine Valters Paintner, of the Abbey of the Arts in Ireland, writes that breath prayer gives us the gift of presence, stability and gratitude.[30] It is the simplest constant in our lives. A reminder of the spirit, present with us, one with us, as constant as our breath.

Tonglen: the Buddhist Practice of the Exhale

Breathe in the positive. Let go of what no longer serves. Whether we are on the yoga mat or being coached through a moment of anxiety, the call to expand our lungs with an inhalation of positive energy feels basic to centering practices. It makes sense. We fill ourselves with life-giving air. We draw it into our beings, and it expands us. We pause. We let go of the oxygen-depleted breath and along with it we release tension and negative thoughts. The focus is almost always on the nourishing swell of the inhale. What if we could change our exhale? What if the exhale carried the power of the positive?

Buddhist nun Pema Chödrön writes about the Buddhist understanding of *bodhichitta*: the awareness of connecting with our difficult emotions (pain, rage, fear, loss, grief, isolation, shame) in order to awaken to the suffering of the world and our desire to alleviate that suffering. She says, 'When we arouse *bodhichitta*, we commit to overcoming everything that obscures our innate wisdom and warm-heartedness, everything that cuts us off from our natural ability to empathize with and benefit others.'[31] Our practice of connecting with our own suffering allows us to be of benefit to others. She explains that we can awaken this *bodhichitta* through a very simple practice called *tonglen*. And in this practice the power of the breath is in the exhale.

> We breathe in our pain, and breathe out strength.
> Then we expand this to breathe in the pain of others,
> those we know and those we do not.
> Those who might be suffering exactly what we are.
> We breathe in their pain, and breathe out wellbeing to them.
> We breathe in heaviness. We breathe out light.
> In this meditative practice, we connect ourselves to all beings through our exhale. We change the perspective of the exhale, which now becomes the positive and life-connecting flow.
> We breathe in grief and heartache.

And breathe out peace, moments of joy, and remembrance.
We breathe in pain. And breathe out comfort and wellness.
We breathe in fear and the gripping squeeze of anxiety.
And we breathe out safety and relief.
We breathe in emptiness and loneliness.
And we breathe out wholeness and connectedness.

And as we expand our circles, those to whom we are sending the positive power of our exhalations become one with our breath. They become nameless and only breath.

While you are reading, take a moment to settle into this pattern of breathing. You do not need to get to the end of the chapter. Or to finish whatever is on your list to do right now. Perhaps the most important thing that happens today is becoming aware of your breath. And at any moment when you either feel that prayer does not work for you, or you do not understand what prayer is, or do not make time for prayer in your life, remember, it need only be a breath.

In one breath you can send something positive to yourself.
To those you love.
To those who are in pain.
To all who suffer.
You can connect yourself to all beings.
You bring yourself into alignment with the eternal breath of the spirit.

This is prayer.
I do not ask God to heal others so they will be well.

I understand my connection to others
that we might hold one another's pain.
To be the something greater than us.
That they might feel the power of my exhale,
In their inhale.
And that connection – for me, that is God.

Anáil na Beatha: The Breath of Life

One of the Gaelic words for breath, *anáil*, used in the phrase 'the breath of life', referring to that which infuses our daily actions with a mixture of work and worship, traces its origin through Arabic and Persian roots back to the Sanskrit word नीला 'dark blue'). It describes the blue of the sky. The sky which holds the deep peace of the flowing air. When we hold our face to the beaming sun or the lashing rain and open our lungs, they are filled with *beatha* the breath of life.[32] The Celtic tradition, indigenous to Scotland and many parts of Europe, sought a deep connection with the divine through creation and the natural world. And through the experiences of daily life. Columba, the 6th-century CE monk who carried Christianity from Ireland to the Isle of Iona off the west coast of Scotland, encountered the indigenous spirituality of the Celtic and Druidic traditions. Here, in time to come, was birthed a beautiful form of practice that honored a trinitarian God through the lens of the already deeply rooted Celtic approach. Prayers that recognize God among us, beside us, before us and above us still resound during worship in this thin place.

Pilgrims to the island to this day slip easily into the rhythm of prayer of the Iona Community, where they find guests and community members in the abbey church at nine o'clock in the morning and nine in the evening. The prayers often reflect a global perspective – lifting up people and places around the world, and honoring the international community that shapes and sustains Iona's ministry. Every Monday the evening prayers are for justice and peace. Each evening's prayers are shaped by the theme of prayer for that day. When I first arrived there for an extended period of time, I strategized which services I would attend to give myself the time I needed for my own practices. But as the weeks progressed, I found that missing a service felt like missing a breath. *Anáil na beatha*, the breath of life. The repetition, the rhythm, the act of showing up at 9am and 9pm felt like breathing itself.

In this following prayer attributed to Columba, I give you his Latin so that you might experience how good the repetition feels. The rhythm is apparent even visually, even if you do not know how to pronounce or translate Latin. But reading it aloud, listening to it, grammatically, there is a cadence. Perhaps the intention was to center our heartbeats and breathing in prayer, or perhaps the pattern mirrors our heartbeats and our breathing. The repetitive structure of prayers deeply influenced by Celtic practices holds within it the lapping of waves on rocks, the flapping wings of wild geese, the drumming of rain, and the echoing footsteps of centuries of pilgrims.

> Adiutor laborantium,
> Bonorum rector omnium,
> Custos ad propugnaculum,
> Defensorque credentium,
> Exaltator humilium,
> Fractor superbientium,
> Gubernator fidelium,
> Hostis impoenitentium,
> Iudex cunctorum iudicum,
> Castigator errantium,
> Casta vita viventium,
> Lumen et pater luminum.
> Attributed to St. Columba (6th c. CE)

> Helper of workers,
> Ruler of all good things,
> Guard at the defence,
> And defender of those trusting,
> Lifter of the low,
> Humbler of the proud,
> Navigator of the faithful,
> Enemy of the impenitent,
> Judge of all who judge,
> Corrector of those who wander,
> Pure life of the living,
> Light and creator of lights.

From the Inner Hebrides to the Outer Hebrides, from the 6th century to the 19th century, where we find the prayer of Mary Macrae, who lived as a cottar on the island of Harris. She had no formal training. She was simply living her life and using the Gaelic native to these lands. The pattern of Christian prayer infused with the rhythm of the Celtic ways becomes a pattern for how she lives. Every action finds God with her and herself with God. In this form of prayer, repetitive motions of daily work, pulling in fishing lines, hanging the washing, weaving, stirring the pot, hammering the nails, every action becomes a prayer. Every breath becomes a prayer.

> DIA liom a laighe,
> Dia liom ag eirigh,
> Dia liom anus gach rath soluis,
> Is gun mi rath son as aonais,
> Gun non rath as aonais.
> Criosda liom a cadal,
> Criosda liom a dusgadh,
> Criosda liom a caithris,
> Gach la agus oidhche,
> Gach aon la is oidhche.
> Dia liom a comhnadh
> Domhnach liom a riaghladh,
> Spiorad liom a treoradh,
> Gu soir agus siorruidh,
> Soir agus siorruidh, Amen.
> Triath nan triath, Amen.
>
> Mary Macrae, 1866 [33]

> God with me lying down,
> God with me rising up,
> God with me in each ray of light,
> Nor I a ray of joy without him,
> Nor one ray without him.
> Christ with me *sleeping*,
> Christ with me *waking*,

> Christ with me *watching*,
> Every day and night,
> Each day and night.
> God with me *protecting*,
> The Lord with me *directing*,
> The Spirit with me *strengthening*,
> Forever and for evermore,
> Ever and evermore, Amen.
> Chief of chiefs, Amen.

Mary Macrae, in her prayer, calls God's presence into her life and also calls us into the practice of recognizing the divine in every moment and every aspect of life, 'nor one ray without him'. I gathered a group of those exploring what prayer means to them during a session of Alignment and offered them Mary Macrae's pattern of prayer. A group of people finding community on Zoom loaded the chat with the divine presence they found in the places where they were sitting in front of a computer screen. A far cry from the shores of a Hebridean island, but every bit as present.

> God with me embracing as I mourn.
> God with me strengthening as I heal.
> God with me releasing, as I discern.
> God with me cleaning, as I walk the spaces of my home.
> G-d with me stretching as I rest my body.
> G-d with me navigating as I journey along this path.
> God with me swaying as I soar with the music.
> God with me calming as I am restless.
> God with me dwelling as I enjoy the peace of a late summer's eve.
> God with me thanking as I collect the last of the season's produce.
> God with me blessing as I feel the love for this sacred circle.
> God with me holding my cat as I feel her warm fur.
> God with me hydrating as I remember to give my body
> the water it needs to function.
> God with me cheering as I am able to embrace new friends.
> God with me creating as I prepare my classes

for the new school year.
God with me encouraging as I try my hand at painting.
God with me rejoicing as I await the birth of my daughter's daughter.
G!d with me unfolding as I explore this world.
God with me settling as I sink into the comfort
of a shared time of prayer.
G!d with me nourishing as I absorb my evening meal.
God with me relishing as I inhale the calming fragrance of lavender.
God with me delighting as I listen to the sounds of the birds.
G-d with me forgiving as I become my best self.
God with me presenting abundance as I contemplate my to-do list.
G!d with me so gently as I am impatient.
God with me thanking, as I am grateful for all my sisters.
God with me relaxing as I listen to the sounds of the clearing
of our evening meal.
God with me slowing as I feel the change in my breathing.

I invite you to find this rhythm of prayer for yourself:

God with me _____ing, as I _____.

Practice

LOVING WORDS

Our two words for breathing in English, inspiration and inhalation, are both rooted in Latin words. *Spirare*: the rushing, blowing breathing that enters with purpose. *Halare*: that gives us our inhale and exhale, the natural flow of air that comes without any intention other than just being. May our prayers be filled with both. Filled with the spirit that rushes into our dry bones and gives us life. And balanced with an inhale and exhale, both rooted in the life-giving energy of connectedness.

In my Latin class, gathered in a circle on the floor, we called in the spirit of the Musa. *Musa mihi fabulam memora*. Muse, remember the story for me. With a giant inhale, I received the story of those who went before us. The story passed on to another group of students, who will perhaps hold it tightly and pass it on themselves one day. In one breath, the Muse inspires. Here again, the focus is on the intake of the breath. The inspiration. It gives us the story. But what is this story if not shared? The beauty of the oral tradition that has given us everything from the Torah to the Odyssey to the Tao Te Ching is in the passing on of the story. When the inhale becomes exhale, the connection is made. From those past to those yet to be. From me to you. From life-receiving to life-giving.

It fills us with the narrative of our life. And with the stories of all those who have breathed that same air.

RETHINK

Prayer is as simple as a breath.

REFRAME

As you take moments in the day to notice your inhales and exhales, also be aware that they connect to every other living thing that experiences the flow of air, even the stones that feel the breath of wind brushing past them.

REIMAGINE

Consider that in the sharing of your story, in the naming (with words or not) those in the circles of your life, your every exhale is connected to someone's inhale. Breathe your *hesed*, your loving kindness, breathe your *anáil*, your breath of life, to all beings.

Chapter 10
Naming God

Practice
The names of God
As the names of the trees.

Being Named

Sitting on the floor surrounded by thirty postcards of different types of frogs and toads, my two-year-old son delighted in picking up a card and announcing the name. American toad! Poison dart frog! The applause and cheers of his amazed parents fueled this favorite pre-dinner routine. Such brilliance we had never seen in a wee thing that couldn't yet poop in the potty. There was comfort as well as delight in naming things. From his first identification of family members to the names of the dinosaurs in his favorite book, it was a sign that he was ready to explore the world. To name it and be a part of it. To dive into the world with awareness and joyful recognition.

When I visited my brother recently on the beautiful wooded piece of land where he lived, I was reminded that we too had grown up with a love of naming what was around us. A practice instilled in us by our parents no doubt, the ritual of going around the garden and naming all of the plants, the joy of sharing the names, of knowing each plant. I couldn't wait for the morning to have the tour of my brother's vegetable beds and to hear the name of each sprouting plant, lovingly tended. We walked in the woods, naming all the trees, using an app to figure out the unknown ones. My brother told me a friend asked him, 'Why do you have to name all the trees?' Do other families not do this?

My garden is always filled with herbs. In spring when first the perennials grow green and into fall when sprigs are gathered for drying, my daily prayer is saying their names.

Chives, chamomile, dill, fennel.
Parsley, sage, rosemary, thyme, English and lemon.
Lemon verbena and lemon balm, spearmint.

Echinacea, bee balm. oregano, basil, lavender.
Each one has its own smell and taste and particular look.
Some are hard to tell apart at first until you touch them
and rub them with your fingers, releasing their scent.
Some come back every year, some die off after a few years,
and some I plant fresh every spring.
But what is that great delight I have in standing there
and naming them all?
That same joy in knowing the names of the trees. And the birds.
And the frogs. And the dinosaurs.
What is that love of capturing the identities?

Perhaps it is our way of seeking that direct relationship with the divine that we crave from prayer. Of knowing God so closely that we can call God by name. In Muslim Sufi practice the names of Allah (swt) are repeated as a form of prayer called *dhikr*. A remembrance of God. A form of prayer that creates connection with the divine through the naming of all the ways in which God is known to us. The *dhākir*, the one who recites these prayers, is reminding their heart of God, until their heart reminds them of God. The ninety-nine names of Allah (swt) are sung in a *nasheed* or counted with fingers rolling over beads. Asheq Fazlullah tells a story of his father watching his uncle sound asleep, his lips mouthing the *dhikr* in his sleep. He had reminded his heart of these names in prayer to the point that even asleep, his heart reminded him of them. God present in his every breath.

Do we name the things in the world around us also in a form of *dhikr*? We see the divine in the myriad forms of plant and animal life, in the beauty and complexity of species, in the diversity of life, God in unlimited form, and in bountiful presence, vibrantly alive in everything that we can name.

Hineni

'Here I am,' said the Hebrew prophet Isaiah. 'Send me.'[34] What a statement of complete and utter humility.

Readiness. Willingness. Vulnerability.
Here I am. Send me.

The prophet Isaiah in the Hebrew scriptures has seen the glory of the Lord. He has had some sort of experience with winged seraphs, a vision of something so huge that he can only see the hem of its robe filling the temple. He has felt worthless and been released from that with a cleansing coal on his lips. Some experience has moved him so deeply that when he felt there was work to be done, called by God, he said, 'Here I am. Send me.'

And in this action he becomes the voice of God for the people. The voice of the people for God. He becomes the connection between humanity and divinity. A prophet. He names himself and offers himself as a visible, tangible, knowable connection between God and God's people.

Here I am. One word, *hineni,* in Hebrew. This one word enters story after story in the Hebrew scriptures. As someone responds to a call, fulfils their part of a covenantal connection between God and humanity. Someone being called to service or leadership. The prophets and keepers of the covenant. Abraham responds to God with this word, and then Jacob, and Joseph, and Moses. Samuel responds three times – Here I am. *Hineni.*

And then it bleeds into the beginning of the Gospel of Luke when the angel appears to Mary and announces that she will give birth to the son of God. Luke puts a Greek version of these words into her mouth. Here I am. The servant of the Lord. May it be for me according to your word. This word, or phrase as it is translated, is emblematic of a response to a call from God.

But

It is *God* that says it more often than the prophets and leaders of the people. The writers of these texts put this word into God's voice over and over. *Hineni.*

And

The translators of these texts erase it from God's mouth.

Translations have God say: I'll do this and I'll do that. But it's the same word, *hineni,* here I am ... to do this or that. It is God who first uses this expression. To Noah in establishing the covenant, God says here I am. In Hebrew, not in English. Over and over again God meets the people with the words here I am. Only late in Isaiah is it once attributed to God. *Then you shall call, and the Lord will answer; you shall cry for help, and God will say, Here I am. Hineni.*[35] The writers of our scriptures create a call and response out of these words, something we do not get to see in translation.

A call and response. The very thing we are trained to understand as prayer. In our deepest, darkest times, all we want to hear is that 'Here I am' from that something bigger than us. Even when we feel as if we are trying our hardest, fighting our strongest battles with health or work or grief or addiction. Trying our hardest, bringing our here-I-am every day. And all we need is to hear it back. A here-I-am from God. This is where a traditional understanding of prayer can set us up for thinking that prayer doesn't work. When we do not hear those words.

Could the translators be on to something? That we might not get to hear those exact words descending on us like a coating balm for our pain. That God is not going to text back with a reply to our call. But that in naming God, in calling out to God in prayer, we can see and hear and touch and feel the response in the blossoming of the bud, the regrowth of the perennial, the majesty of the tree, and the gentle swish of the bird flying from branch to branch.

So what is that love of capturing the identities, of naming things?

I think it's our craving for God's *hineni*. They are all God's *hineni*. Here I am. Know me in the song of that bird. In the name of the herb. In the type of tree. In the smell of that flower. In the wind that blows and you don't know where it comes from or where it's going.

Here I am. Here I am. See me. Know me. Name me.

It's that covenantal connection.

That need to know and be known.

To name and be named.

This poem by Rainer Maria Rilke speaks to the knowing of God that we crave, the understanding of connection that we seek.

> *I find you, Lord, in all Things and in all*
> *my fellow creatures, pulsing with your life;*
> *as a tiny seed you sleep in what is small*
> *and in the vast you vastly yield yourself.*

> *The wondrous game that power plays with Things*
> *is to move in such submission through the world:*
> *groping in roots and growing thick in trunks*
> *and in treetops like a rising from the dead.*

Rilke notices not just that God is to be seen and known and named in all things, but that God's power is to move in submission through the world. To say – here I am. See me in the growing leaves on a knotted and broken tree. Hear me in the rain against the window, in the lapping of the waves, in the sounds that we ignore because we are so busy filling this space with words. In the naming is the noticing of the *hineni* of the divine. God whispers these words in all of creation. The whisper of these words in all creation is God. We are one with this submissive power that maybe offers us nothing more than presence. Here I am. And perhaps that's all we need from our God.

Breathing the Name of God

In Jewish tradition the very name of the divine is synonymous with breath. The tetragrammaton, the four-letter two-syllable sound for YHWH, is thought to be the inhale and exhale of the limitless name: I am who I am, I will be who I will be. The opening verse of the Nishmat Kol Chai prayer calls on the name of God from all beings that breathe.

נִשְׁמַת כָּל חַי

תְּבָרֵךְ אֶת שִׁמְךָ

יְהֹוָה אֱלֹהֵינוּ.

The breathing soul of all life
Will bless your name
Adonai/YHWH, our God.

Father Richard Rohr tells a story of the rabbi who taught him this prayer. 'The Jews did not speak God's name, but breathed it with an open mouth and throat: inhale—Yah; exhale—weh. By our very breathing we are speaking the name of God and participating in God's breath. This is our first and our last word as we enter and leave the world.'[36] We take in the breath that utters the name of the limitless one. We exhale the breath that is the completion of the name. The extension of the divine into the world, from us to all living and breathing beings. We are the breath of the divine, and in our praise and in our lament, we exhale.

If our prayers are a seeking of connection with the one through whom we know and experience life, then surely we know the name of that one as our breath alone. As Thich Nhat Hanh reminds us, in naming God we have already limited God. But in breathing God, perhaps we are naming God in an unlimiting way, as part of the essence of life, our life and the life of all living things. Even the things over which we breathe that might not have breath themselves. Like a toddler who delights in discovering proper nouns, naming and claiming the world around them, may we know the name of God in all the wonders we can name and in every breath. The breaths that produce words and the ones that simply keep us alive.

Practice

LOVING WORDS

That Greek word in the New Testament for *hineni*: ἰδού, idou. It is an imperative (command) form of a verb that means 'to see' (ὁράω, horao) but has more of the flavor of 'to be sure to see' or 'to see something so you can be sure about it'. Translations of it are usually something like *Behold* or *Lo*. It's all over the New Testament. My seminary Greek professor, Dr. Eric Heen, had a much better translation for it. One without words. It was a heavy slap of his hand on the table. As his students, when we came to one of the many verses that we were translating from Greek that began with this word, he had us slap our hand on the table instead of trying to put it into words. A gesture that communicated 'Hey, see here, pay attention to this.'

It feels a long cry from the submissive-sounding response to a call, *hineni*, here I am. Let it be with me according to your word.

So to trace the journey of this expression:

- Hebrew *hineni* was used by God and those called by God
- Translators into English removed it from the mouth of God in favor of the words 'I'll do this for you.'
- Writers of the New Testament in Greek use the word *idou* in a similar context.
- Translators into English use the words 'Behold', 'Lo', and 'Here I am' to translate it.
- But the Greek word has taken on more of a tone of immediacy, attention and verification than of response and submission.

So what does this all say about prayer? I think it speaks volumes about the human desire for God to see us and know us. See me. Hear me. I'm here. *Idou* is like a prayer that cries out from the depths of our humanity, needing connection to the divine. A slap on the table. But if we trace the *hineni* back to its original Hebrew, it is a gentle reminder that there is a conversation, a presence, an answering that may not be heard (or translated) yet is there. Prayer need not be a call and response. It might only be a remembrance, a *dhikr*, that when we call on the name of God, God has already called our name.

RETHINK ...

prayer as a simple naming of everything we encounter in creation.

REFRAME

As we seek communication and connection from prayer, let us see that connection through naming. Naming God by the ways the divine is revealed to us in the world. Knowing God in and through the collection of creation. Reminding our hearts of God's presence in all things and times. And in our breath alone.

REIMAGINE ...

walking through a garden as an act of prayer. Imagine a walk through the woods and the naming of the trees as an act of *dhikr*. Imagine being free enough to know God without name and with all names.

Chapter 11
The Journey of Identity

Practice
the sound of your name
as if it were not a word

Gender Identity

For decades I asked my students on the first day of Latin class if they were a *discipulus* or a *discipula*, gathering the information, and then playing with the plurals as I prompted them to figure out the difference in their first gendered inflections in an ancient language. I did not appreciate how inappropriate and limiting the exercise was until I came to understand I was in a classroom of students who had a more open awareness of their gender identity, a number of whom opted to use a beautiful range of non-gendered pronouns. I began to offer a third option, a fabricated nominative singular, *discipulum*. A neuter form, not masculine or feminine. Ne-uter, I told them. Not either. The Latin language had this figured out long before our clumsy English came along. At first I was wary of presenting a word that they would not find in the compendium of Latin literature, a non masculine or feminine student, feeling as though I was stepping outside of my duty to preserve what was given to us by the ancients. It proved, however, to be much more meaningful to demonstrate the potential of this language to be inclusive of those who do not identify within the gender binary that our English language offers.

When we first renamed the one bathroom in our middle school building that was not labeled Boys or Girls, a plaque on the door said Gender Neutral Bathroom. I balked at the wording. Were we stripping these students of having any gender at all just because they did not identify as male or female? I asked the administration to change the sign to read All Gender which they did quickly, even before any students saw the first attempt. We have lost the beauty of the Latin word neuter. In English the word neuter sanitizes gender, whereas I feel comfortable explaining to students that the roots of this word hold the understanding of a non-binary identification. Simply, not either. It opens us to the spectrum. We lost the beauty of this word and the opportunity offered by it.

Alongside my Latin courses, I taught a course called Prima Lingua, a program I developed to give students the opportunity to learn about how languages work, which they took before beginning the formal study of one language. Generally used by 10- to 12-year-old students, it was a study of the development of language itself and systems of writing. We explored language families and traced the development of words. The heart of the course focused on grammatical structures and linguistic patterns that are common to many world languages, such as adjective agreement and placement, verb conjugations, and yes, gendered nouns. To structure the course, we looked at these patterns mainly in Latin and compared them to how English handles the same, before exploring the patterns in other languages. We created our own spectrum of languages with a highly inflected Latin at one end and a minimally inflected English at the other, and then noticed that other languages often fall somewhere along this spectrum of inflection.

For years it was a matter of course to explain to students that a chair was feminine, not because of any biological nature, but mainly because all nouns are assigned a gender. We always had a laugh at the Romans who could not bear first declension *agricola*, *poeta*, and *nauta* (farmer, poet, sailor) to take the feminine gender of their declension counterparts. Natural gender was a given for words like *rex* and *pater* (king, father), masculine because of their nature. But the topic of gendered nouns in different languages broke open the possibility of discussing the bias held in such terms as 'natural gender' – and gave me the opportunity to use this dead language to support a growing number of students who were aware of the power that languages hold to enable us to understand our own identities.

In a Latin poetry class with older students, we were similarly opened to an awareness of how an author engenders a response in us, the readers of an ancient text, with the use of rhetorical devices. Synecdoche makes us focus on the part that represents the whole, like the opening word of Virgil's great epic, the *arma* that represent basically the entirety of Aeneas's experience. Our minds are primed for conflict. The Latin student, with lists of literary devices in tow, learns to identify everything from an anastrophe to a zeugma and to analyze the purpose of their inclusion. The device that allowed me to use the ancient texts to support my LGBTQIA++ students, who made it past the days of shaking their heads at the fact that *dux* (leader) is considered to have natural gender, is called *merism*. It is a rhetorical device that etymologically refers to a cutting and separating between two opposites, but which at its heart upholds the very spectrum that we are seeking in a gender-inclusive society.

Simple examples of merism help us illustrate the device. We searched *near* and *far* to find the answer. The use of this common merism does not mean, of course, that we looked in the places that were near and then the places that were far, but implies the totality of everything along that spectrum. The moving passage in Virgil's Aeneid[37] about the creature Fama (Rumor) is replete with uses of merism. She moves *nocte* (at night) and *luce* (in the light) in the middle of the *caeli* (sky) and *terrae* (land). Virgil's use of merism depicts the personification of rumor as all-encompassing in time and space. We cannot escape the detrimental effects of rumor and the havoc it wreaks in our lives. But in addition to the appreciation of the imagery and emotional response induced, we have learned that there was a literary device that literally supported the concept of the totality created by naming the opposites of a binary.

Perhaps there is hope to be found here for our non-binary students who see themselves as an afterthought in the canon of our language structures, who have had to educate the world on the pronouns that work and do not work for them. And perhaps these same students can take their newfound knowledge of an ancient language back to their faith communities and ask their priests, ministers and rabbis to re-examine the beginning of Bereshit, of Genesis, of the description of the creation of humanity, this text most likely written when the Jews were in exile in Babylon, encountering other peoples that had their own creation stories, feeling the need to have a creation story of their own. God names darkness and light, day and night, heaven and earth, male and female. Surely, surely, these powerful examples of merism were already opening the world to the totality of human expression. That which is male and female and then the unlimited expanse of everything that is not either. Created by a God whose grammatical identifiers are plural. And Elohim (pl) said, Let *us* make humankind in *our* image. (Gen 1:26)

So when we turn to prayer, experimenting with the ways in which we name the divine, perhaps we can also try out new names for ourselves. Prayer might be just the place to do this. To see ourselves as the spectrum of identities that we carry. The merism that we are.

Seeing God Face to Face

One of the fascinating things about the process of writing is that you are coming to know me better through reading this, but I am only imagining you, my reader, in this relationship. I have the practice of holding you in prayer as I write, hoping that you are reading something that feels meaningful, that strikes a chord for you in some way, that resonates. I hold you present with me, you in all of your identities. The questioner. The seeker. The mourner. The curious. The lost. The hungry. The empty. The well-wisher. The nay-sayer. The pray-er. The reader.

Perhaps we know each other already. Perhaps we will meet some day. Or perhaps we will only know each other through the experience of this book, the writing and the imagined reading of it. But will we emerge from this encounter changed?

In every relationship that we have, we lug around a satchel with all of the other encounters we have had in our lives up to this point. Ways in which we identify ourselves from these encounters. Ways in which we are known, or not. But what if we were able to strip ourselves of all of those identities and histories that we carry, to approach the relationship we seek in prayer in some raw form, to meet God face to face. And to emerge changed.

Jacob, son of Rebekah and Isaac, brother of Esau, had just such an experience as recounted in the Hebrew scriptures. A pivotal moment in his life. We come to know Jacob in some really compromising positions in these ancient stories. We first meet him as he is grabbing the heel of his brother in the womb. Not the firstborn, not the bearer of the birthright blessing, but desperately grabbing for it even in utero. We travel with his story as his mother encourages him to deceive his brother Esau and his dying father. A dysfunctional family story at best.

But then Jacob comes to the river Jabbok. He strips himself of everything. Jabbok and Jacob with just the last two consonants reversed. It's a crafty piece of writing, laden with interesting literary tricks like this. Jabbok means the place of *wrestling*, and it's the place where Jacob's name will be changed to Israel, the one who *wrestled* with God. The text plays with names and lack of names, and meaning of names, but then ultimately there's the stripping away of things that have identified Jacob. At the river, Jacob lets go of all those histories and encounters that have defined him to this point. His wives and eleven children, marking him as the one who moves the line of God's people forward. His servants, divesting himself of his position of power. And finally everything that he had. He is likely naked and alone and stripped of all that gave him a sense of self. And here he meets this stranger in the night.

In this moment Jacob has to come to terms with who he is. The stealer and the carrier of the blessing, the one who has manipulated and been manipulated. A brother who is about to come face to face with the brother that he cheated. He has to come to terms with all that he is and let it go, so that he can come face to face with God. And emerge changed. A new name, a new blessing, and an identity that names him as all of the people of God, Israel.

So at its core, this is a story about identity. Owning all that it is but also realizing that stripped of everything we carry, in our most raw form, we are inseparable from our identification with God. From Jacob and Jabbok, words twisted together, to two characters literally wrestling in the night whose pronouns make them indistinguishable, Jacob meets God face to face, in the barest essence of who he is, and emerges transformed.

The struggle with identity and our relationship with the divine is most certainly not unique to any one tradition. The Bhagavad Gita, part of the sacred epic of Hindu scripture, which was written at just about the same time as Genesis, lists all the ways in which our satchel is filled with identities.[38] Ones that come from the family we are connected to, the communities we are a part of, our cultural and religious affiliations, the work that we do, the causes that we stand up for. But the Hindu teaching says we should set aside all these identities because they are transient and the cause of bondage, delusion and suffering. As long as we are caught up in them, we cannot know our true spiritual identity as the eternal, indestructible and infinite Self. In Hinduism our spiritual identity is the most important of all our identities, because it is our permanent and independent identity that cannot be altered. What I find really fascinating is that this identity is so closely linked to the divine, they are so one and the same that we can't even understand or name them separately. It is the first word of the Guru Granth Sahib, the sacred scripture of Sikhism, Ik Onkar, the oneness of God and all humanity that Valarie Kaur writes about so beautifully.

It is exactly how Jacob walks with the limp in his hip. His encounter with God literally embedded in the way he walks. The limp that he walks away from Jabbok with is not an infirmity. It is a symbol that the way he walks through life and his new name (isra-EL) are inextricably bound to God. Everything stripped away, he and God live as one. Now he really gets that blessing. The blessing that God walks with him. And in this state, he is able to encounter his brother Esau again. This time, when he sees Esau, he says it is like seeing the face of God. In seeing God face to face, as a result of this encounter, this wrestling, he is able to see God in the face of even his most feared adversary.

Kaitlin Curtice, a member of the Potawatomi nation of Turtle Island, is a storyteller, a poet, and the author of a number of deeply moving books, including one called *Native: Identity, Belonging, and Rediscovering God* in which she grapples with the issue of identity as it relates to the broadening of our understanding of God. In this book she says, 'Identity does not come to us without journey, because to learn who we are means we face difficult truths in our own lives and imagine what life might look like as those truths work themselves out inside of us.'[39] I can't help but think of Jacob when I read her words – Jacob facing his difficult truths and undergoing the internal struggle that we see dramatized as wrestling with God. This wrestling, for me, reflects not only a moment of spiritual crisis but a moment of transformation, of identity being reformed in divine encounter. It resonates with the Hindu understanding of the self as something inseparable from the divine – identity not as fixed, but as something braided together with God through struggle, reflection and growth.

And here is where Kaitlin says it, that phrase that puts it all into perspective for me: 'Our work is to call each other home, to call to one another's spirits and say, This is what it means to be human, to love and be loved.'[40] Our work is to call each other home.

> Home
> Where the me that has no name
>   and that has a satchelful of names
> Meets the divine which has no name
>   and an infinite cosmos of names
> To wrestle with the pulse points of pain
> The shifting balance of growth and decline
> The opening awareness of self and of other
> To emerge changed
> To find that home has become the place where we are known
> As everything and as nothing
> But as inseparable from one another.

Practice

LOVING WORDS

A little more on merism. One of the reasons I believe poetry to be the richest literary art form is because of the rhetorical, or literary, devices that poets use to convey messages, like hidden treasure among the verses. Poetry read aloud that makes use of alliteration or assonance evokes a response caused by the sounds of the words. Meter can be used to convey the tone of a line as Virgil so skillfully does throughout the Aeneid.

<u>Multa quoque et bello passus</u> dum conderet urbem
<u>Also having suffered many things in war</u> until he would found a city
Each underlined syllable in Latin carries a long, stressed weight in the reading of it.

But merism, a lesser known of the devices, has probably had more of an impact on our belief systems that we might understand. The device that cuts apart two ends of a spectrum, but in the use of it, refers to the entirety of the spectrum. A verse in the Revelation of John from the Christian canon practically defines merism.

> *Also it causes all, both small and great, both rich and poor, both free and slave, to be marked on the right hand or the forehead, so that no one can buy or sell unless he has the mark, that is, the name of the beast or the number of its name.* (Revelation 13:16-17)

The use of the structure καὶ...καὶ, both...and, is set against the bookmarking words πάντας (all) and μή τις (no one). Both/and creates the cutting, and all/no one defines the totality. A pretty amazing verse written by John who was hugely influenced by the Roman writing of his time, including Virgil's pivotal work as the first poet laureate of his day. And an epic that shaped the path of understanding empire.

To appreciate sacred scriptures, from a wide span of space and time and tradition and language, is to open us to what merism offers. An expanse of understanding. The breadth that is held in the simple naming of opposites. The beauty of gender expression that was understood by the ancients and welcomed and upheld in biblical literature. The possibility of meeting both ourselves and God at the intersection of all points on the spectrum.

RETHINK ...

the ways in which language shapes our understanding of God and of ourselves.

REFRAME

We are as unlimited as the divine which we name without any certainty as well as in a million different ways.

REIMAGINE

Can prayer become a way of reimagining ourselves – embracing the fullness of our identities, with all their intersections and complexities? A way of offering who we are to the divine, as revealed not only within us, but also in the vibrant diversity of the world around us.

Chapter 12

Claiming and Reclaiming

Practice
Claiming the darkness
As the arrival of peace

Turning to Our Pagan Roots

My dear friend Barbara Chaapel is a poet. But I have had to convince her to claim that identity. To name herself as a poet. When offering her bio for presentations, she first lists her professional positions as clergy. Born into a time when she had to claim her rightful place as a pastor and preacher among a sea of black-robed men, she is well-deserving of uplifting her fifty plus years in ordained ministry at the top of her *curriculum vitae*. But for me, the most important work that Barbara does is poetry. Are we brave enough to call this a vocation and not an avocation in our world? For those who are not publishing books and making money from their writing, can we uphold poets as those who open our eyes and hearts and minds to the unnoticed, in ways that transform our perspective? Barbara is a poet. And she is also a crone.

Although I grew up with the Celtic echoes of Iona reverberating through my Christian practices, the identification with pagan tradition was not honored in Christian communities as it seems to be today. The limited understanding of what was pagan referenced only what was outside of the Church. Heathen. Cultish. My Scottish Presbyterian upbringing pointed me to John Calvin and John Knox as my guides for what was to be done decently and in order. At times I felt it might be more important to follow Reformed theologian Karl Barth than Jesus Christ.

Barbara and I paid a visit one fall afternoon to Columcille, a megalith park in the mountainous Poconos region of Pennsylvania. Walking in the shadow of the giant stones, which feel as if they were placed there by wayward Druids, Barbara told me that she had attended a ritual in these woods during which she claimed the identity of crone. This waning phase of womanhood marks the time of life for the Triple

Goddess when wisdom and experience surface as the guiding light. To walk with Barbara through the woods is to stop every few steps to name the bird that has just flown overhead, a ruby-crowned kinglet, an Eastern phoebe. To touch the berries hanging full on the branches of the bush passed by. To bend down to greet the passing dog and share a story with its owner of rescues and fostering. Time spent connecting with the treasures that are sometimes too common to notice. And then, when the day is over, a poem comes. The wisdom and experience of the crone is planted into words that take shape and translate images into phrases. The poems are texted or emailed. Sometimes they are written just for me. For her. For those who walk together. Each one a gift. Each one a prayer that looks at God's creation through the eyes of a crone.

More and more, I see Christian leaders turning to their pagan roots, welcoming the solstice into their Christmas celebrations with rituals of lights and candles and solstice labyrinth walks. At Columcille Megalith Park, Christian, Pagan and Wiccan leaders gather for a sunrise solstice observation. They recognize the longing for light as one of the basic needs of humanity. Light just might need its own spot on Maslow's Hierarchy of Needs along with shelter, safety and love. For as long as people have gathered in community, they have created ritual to honor the light. Instead of being threatened by what is pagan, Christians are embracing the connection to the human need for worship that is not restricted by orthodoxy.

Widely accepted is the fact that the date of Christmas has its roots in the Roman celebration of the sun and the god Saturn. Early Christians in Rome couched their celebration of the birth of the Messiah in the Saturnalia celebrations that culminated on December 25. And just as these new followers of the Way co-opted the imperial language to describe their leader as Lord, King, Prince of Peace, so they connected the holy day of Christmas to this solstice-time celebration. So isn't it a beautiful thing that Christian leaders now seem increasingly comfortable reconnecting our Christmas celebrations with ancient solstice rituals?

Megan LeCluyse, director of the Christian Association at the University of Pennsylvania, reflects on her visits to Stonehenge and

Orkney. These sites of neolithic sun-worship predate Christianity by 3000 years. She notes the paradox of her path to Christian ministry alongside her resonance with these pagan sites. She recognizes the beauty found in her connection with worshippers who did not know Jesus Christ. They longed for the light in the world as we do. They are part of the same story. It is not a paradox at all. It is Christians awakening to a deeper placement of Christ's story cradled in the story of all creation.

The island of Iona is known as the birthplace of Christianity in Scotland, but from the 6th century of the common era, worshippers here have held the Celtic and Christian worlds in close communion. John Philip Newell, teacher of Celtic spirituality and former warden of the Iona Community, explains that 'the Christ mystery did not seem strange to the Celtic worldview. Rather, it gave further expression to the sacredness the Celts already knew existed deep in the matter of the earth and in the stirring of the human soul.'[41]

Pagan and Christian have been woven into the same fabric for pilgrims to this holy island and for the care for creation that has spread throughout the world from this community. Reclaiming our pagan roots is tantamount to honoring our indigeneity. In the same way that Barbara is a pastor and a preacher, but first she is a poet and a crone.

Saving Solstice

Some Christians like to ponder on what Jesus would have thought. The following poem offers some imaginings of the Christ child, stirring in the womb during the solstice days of darkness. Ready to be light in the world. Ready to embrace those who were in the flesh before him. Their ways of worship. Their longing for light. Had Jesus seen those standing stones, I feel quite certain he would have marveled at their glory. And joined in the dance.

Saving Solstice

> The faeries dance and dreamers pray
> All biding in the shortest day

>   That light will come from out this brew
>   Of cold and dark
>   the winter's stew.
>
> In hope and faith they gather round
> As songs are lifted from the ground
>   To echo in the depths of night
>   'Please rid us of this fearsome blight.
>
> So light will come and life renew
> And earth enliven with the dew
>   Of days grown longer in the sun
>   Come light again. Let us be one.'
>
> But there inside her burdened womb
> Waits one who listens to their tune
>   Their thirst for light, their need for hope
>   Their rituals helping them to cope.
>
> She pushes life into this world
> Her light, made flesh, new hope unfurled.
>   They stop their dance and turn their gaze
>   And put away their common ways.
>
> But no! He shouts into the night.
> Don't stop for me. It isn't right.
> I've come in flesh to join with you
> That darkness might be honored too.

Embracing Darkness

Claiming our roots to traditions that are native to the land from which we come brings us closer to the rhythms of the earth. Our practices of slowing as the days darken pay tribute to those who lived by the turning of the seasons.

I tend to hibernate once the clock changes. My usual walks around the neighborhood are supplanted by a few hours of browsing videos on my phone. My dog is fine just going out back instead of having a lively jaunt. Netflix beckons, and a good book by the fire. There just isn't the same impetus to do anything when the walk back from work is in darkness and bedtime calls early.

The darkness.

The rhythms are slower; the days are shorter; the motivation is low. But if I reclaim my pagan roots, I can reframe the darkness as an important part of my life of prayer.

Barbara Chaapel, in her poem *Let There Be Darkness*, calls us to uphold the darkness and cherish the gifts that it brings.

> Follow me to the hidden cave,
> stand in the cool earth
> under the drippings of stone
> by dark pools of water gems:
>
> Stand still. Breathe.
>
> Crawl with me into the womb,
> warm and wet,
> nourished by rich ruby-blood,
> affixing yourself to life,
> unseeing:
>
> Stand still. Breathe.
>
> Go with me to the black bear's den,
> to curl into the dream,
> heart-slow and happy.
>
> Stand still. Breathe.
>
> Touch my ebony cheeks,
> caress my blue-black fingers,
> drink from the hanging lobes
> of my bronzed breasts and
> name me Mother Africa:
>
> Stand still. Breathe.

Dive with me to the deep sea floor
to live in the hot steam of
earthcore,
in the green darkness of prehistory:

Stand still. Breathe.

Walk with me blind,
as I tap sure steps along the path,
seeing the flowers by their scent,
knowing the mosses by their softness,
hearing the breeze by the ruffling of grasses:

Stand still. Breathe.

Find me standing under winter sky,
Orion hunting overhead,
stars pin-pricking the ink-dark
of December night.

Stand still. Breathe.

Stand still
as the light wanes,
beckons us to darkness
in the night's embrace.
And wait for the turning.

Barbara prompts us to hold the darkness, to embrace the space it offers for reflection. The time that it brings to slow down our pace and let our eyes attune to waning light. The opportunity it gives us to stand still and breathe. We are quick to rush to the light. But let us consider how much richer the darkening time of year would be if we listened to what our bodies and spirits are telling us. Instead of lighting our candles, perhaps we could take time to sit in the dark, forgo that walk, and find a practice that allows us to hold the darkness and stillness. When our bodies cry out for the mindless scrolling on social media and the comfort of the couch, can we recognize the need for a spiritual practice that supports the different hue of these days?

As the light of the day turns golden before you are ready, catch the moment when the sun dips below your view, knowing that it is only out of sight, sure to return again in the morning. It cradles us from beneath and lights the day for our siblings in another part of the world. It is a reminder that in darkness there is sabbath for our bodies. Arriving home from work, feeling as if the day is already over, shed the guilt of tucking into the darkness. In the night's embrace, find the shapes of loneliness, lethargy and loss that come more closely into view in the dark. Hold them and breathe into them.

Awaiting Light

The Hindu Gayatri Mantra has been used to honor the rising and setting of the sun for perhaps 3500 years. The Sanskrit words lead us into the vibrations of the universe that expand beyond light and dark. As we call to one of the deities of the sun, Savitri, we seek clarity in the darkness. We find illumination within ourselves and beyond ourselves in the midst of darkness. The repetition of this mantra allows us to join the limitless *om*, the sound waves that are infinite in time and space. I leave the words untranslated, because it is the repetition, the rhythm, that brings a sense of knowing, closeness, oneness with all creation. Spiritual practice is marked by repetition. And in that repetition comes connection. And in that connection comes a lightening of the loneliness, lethargy and loss. In the darkness we are connected.

> *Om bhuh, bhuvah, swaha*
> *Tat savitur varenyam*
> *Bhargo devasya dhimahi*
> *Dhiyo yo nah prachodayat*

In the Christian calendar the days of darkness before the coming of the light are called Advent. I am frustrated every time I hear an Advent litany that focuses on the meaning of *come*. We await the coming of the Christ child. We await the bringing of the light to the world. But at the root of this beautiful word advent is the Latin meaning of this word –

arrival. As in 'the advent of the internet brought greater connection'.

Advent as arrival feels like a much more powerful use of the word. It beckons us not to wait for the light but to sit in the awareness of what has already arrived in our lives.

To recognize God's presence in the darkness.

Yes, we await the turning. Yes, we long for the light.

But as the darkness descends, let us allow it to hold us

and breathe with us and open us to what lies in the shadows.

The Turning

The Earth continues to turn. Our hibernating hearts and minds embrace that deep longing for spring. The Celts, who were so attuned to the turning of the seasons, knew the importance of the midpoint between the winter solstice and the vernal equinox. The need to hasten the call to warmth and light, to the sprouting of life from hardened ground. Life was lying in wait 'within the womb', *imbolc*. So to the goddess of fire and fertility they called. Brigid, strengthen the heartbeat of the lambs lying curled within their mothers. Ready the milk so that it will flow freely in streams warm and sweet. Crack the hull of seeds that stems might make their way to the surface, ready to peek their heads above the soil. To Brigid they called with fires lit, a step closer to life renewed.

The Celtic goddess Brigid was adopted and adapted by Christians as Brigid of Kildare, whom we met in the liminal space. This holy woman was the midwife of what lay dormant. In the fields and in the barns. In the souls of those who sought connection to themselves and to something greater than themselves. Born to a Christian mother and Druid father, she lived in that sacred space where an understanding of the divine was far more expansive than one way of seeing and knowing. She knew holy ritual in the flowing of the sheep's milk to feed its lamb. She knew that boundaries could not contain a limitless God. She could feel the heartbeat of the divine pulsing in the earth. And she could see the divine lying dormant within every person she met.

The celebration of Imbolc carries me to the powerful prayer offered by Sikh American activist and author Valarie Kaur. She opens her book

See No Stranger by recounting this prayer she offered after the presidential election of 2016 – to a nation in shock More than half of whose citizens felt a wash of darkness cover the Earth. Who didn't know how to wake their children that morning with the news that they did not feel safe.

She prayed with a call to hope. Her call to hope birthed a call to action.

What if this darkness is not the darkness of the tomb, but the darkness of the womb?
What if our America is not dead but a country still waiting to be born? What if the story of America is one long labor …
Remember the wisdom of the midwife: 'Breathe,' she says.
Then: 'Push.'
Now it is time to breathe. But soon it will be time to push.[42]

As we greet the liminal spaces of turning, let us stand with Barbara, with the Brigids and Valarie and all those who know that in these in-between times power and promise lie in wait. As I write this, fires are burning in my nation. Children lie dead in the rubble of war, the *innocenti*. Unspeakable pain festers deep within the bowels of our global community. Can we find what lies dormant, needing to be pushed into being? Can we utter the names of the killers and the killed? Of their families? Of the systems of violence? Do our faith communities allow us to pray for victims and abusers? Could Brigid see the face of the divine even in those who kill the children? Justice lies dormant. We must midwife it into being that it might uncurl itself, unfurl itself, and poke itself above the soil.

Surely the fiery call of Imbolc is not just to sit in patient expectation of what lies unseen, unknown, unbirthed. To wait in pregnant hope. But also to stir the birth pangs. To steady ourselves to labor. That the sweet milk of justice might feed a battered world and that our prayers might be the call to push.

Our traditions have grown from beautiful places that are sometimes overlooked. Forgotten. Claiming our pagan roots is not a turning away but a turning towards the heart of our spiritual practice.

Practice

LOVING WORDS

The crone. The image of the blushing maiden and fertile mother are hardened into the third incarnation of the Triple Goddess in Neopaganism. Even the soft m-sounds of maiden and mother toughen into the guttural crone. The word *crone* is derived from the Latin *caro* (carcass/flesh/meat) whence comes *carrion*, the decaying flesh of an animal. The images are as harsh as the sound of the word itself. Life is hardened at this age? Decaying? Sidling up to the shadow of death. I've often thought it would have been a better option to name the Triple Goddess as Maiden-Mother-Matriarch. But perhaps that is just my need for alliteration. Instead I will turn those Ms upside down and embrace the Witch in this stage of wise womanhood.

My first ceremony with witches was at the Parliament of the World's Religions. Sharing communion with fellow conference participants in an early morning service, there was not enough bread and wine to go around, in a very non loaves-and-fish moment. So the Jewish Kohenet priestesses presiding at the service popped into the Wiccan service in the next room and asked if they could share. In came the witches with bread and apple juice from their ceremony, enough to share with all those in need. Women of wisdom. And a table that was open for all.

RETHINK ...

the importance of claiming our pagan and indigenous heritage.

REFRAME

Let us reclaim the wisdom and experience of holding reverence for the darkness.

REIMAGINE ...

sitting in darkness, slowing the pace, embracing the depth of these moments as an important part of nourishing our wellbeing.

Part Four

Practice Wilderness

Chapter 13
Getting Lost

Practice taking a new path
Allowing yourself to get lost
And when there's no choice but to keep going
                              keep going

Following the Directions

I checked several times that the bus was heading in the right direction. But it wasn't. My daughter, who was coming down with a cold, had handed over the navigation responsibilities to me. To her mother who has no sense of direction. We were in Geneva, about to travel into the Alps where we were releasing the ashes of our beloved surrogate mother/grandmother. Aunt Pat's request was for the earthly remnants of a body that she was done with be taken to the same lake as her husband's, scattered almost a decade before. A lake at the top of a mountain above a small village in the north of Switzerland. A sacred spot that was as close as they could get to heaven, nestled in the clouds and the snowy peaks. Where they walked hand in hand through the years of their lives.

My daughter was born a good traveler. From planning to packing, from making itineraries to enjoying the spontaneous, she has taught me to handle the inevitable wayward moments as opportunities. Except when it comes to my going in the wrong direction. Navigation is one thing she just can't teach me. I have no internal compass. I have a difficult time knowing right from left, much less north from south. And I got us on the bus heading south. Perhaps this could have been one of those wayward opportunities to sightsee in the city, but when you're coming down with a cold and about to scatter a loved one's ashes, and only want to get from A to B, and just need your mother to get you there, getting lost is not an appealing prospect.

But we made it. We stopped for a day and took care of ourselves with a long soak in a thermal bath, followed by a big pot of fondue. And we set out in the right direction the next morning. Feeling a little better, my daughter took over the navigation duties and somehow got us on buses and trains, on a gondola and through a million twists and turns of graveled paths, up and up, till the lake at the top of forever stood before us. And we stood in stillness. In unspeakable awe at the beauty that stretched before us. A glassy expanse of water, cupped in a jagged horizon of snow-capped mountains, their sharp lines piercing the pure blue sky that held eternity before us. Silence. Tears. A prayer with absolutely no words. A liturgy of committal cast aside, not needed, because we were lost in the majesty of the location found.

I made my children go to church every Sunday, in their dressed-up clothes. Just as I had. In the same church. Part of the minister's family. Part of the legacy to uphold. Clinging to traditions. But never had I experienced prayer so truly with my daughter as on that mountaintop. Had I taken them on the wrong bus all those years? Should I have been taking them into the woods every Sunday instead of making sure their shirts were ironed? Yet had they not grown up in that loving community with a sense of belonging to the roots of their ancestors, they would not have had these surrogate parents and grandparents who cherished them, people who taught them that family was more than blood. Now I can only reframe those years as part of a much larger journey. We are not headed or pointed in only one direction. It is time for my children to take over the navigation and to find the experiences that give them a sense of belonging and community, an understanding of awe and wonder, an accountability for finding wellbeing for themselves and their Earth and all those around them. My hope is that they will be comfortable with getting lost along the way.

Rabbi Naomi Levy writes about searching for our soul in her book, *Einstein and the Rabbi*.

> *It's so easy to get lost and confused. Who among us hasn't felt that way? It's so easy for our senses to get dulled – sometimes by a hurt that causes us to shut down, but more often by our routines. We fall into predictable patterns, we get through our days without reaching and stretching and listening. And then you wake up one day and you realize you have drifted far afield from your own essence. You lost yourself while trying to please others. Your work no longer resonates*

with you. *Your relationships feel superficial. With all your obligations and pressures you've stopped doing the things you love. We wander in exile hoping for a way to return to our essence.*[43]

For Rabbi Levy, being lost is akin to a lack of awareness as we make our way through the routines of life. Drifting from our truth and the essence of our being. A dulling of our senses. Lost as directionless. But what if lost is part of the path? The part that helps us to recognize that we must keep going because there is nothing else to do but keep going. When the way is set, the directions clear, and the destination unquestioned, those moments when we stop to take care of ourselves, or pause to notice the possibilities, or reroute and regroup, rethink and reframe, reimagine and regenerate, become less obvious.

Lost is when my senses are heightened. If you allow yourself those moments of being lost, then the questions arise, the world comes into sharper focus, the heart pumps, the multitude of possibilities opens. When one only follows the path set, that is when the dulling happens. We forget the importance of exploring new routes, establishing new traditions, engaging new practices. It is easy to hold fear that we might be going astray, betraying our tradition, being untrue to our roots by branching into new territory. By valuing the moments of being lost, however, we can perhaps engage more clearly with the return to our essence, as Rabbi Levy notes. Then we might come to that mountaintop and find that the prayer that we rehearsed in the pew was a moment on a journey. An important moment on the way to finding something that stretches to forever.

Lost in Prayer

Mirabai Starr leads a contemplative practice of writing for her Holy Lament group each month.

A brief prompt is given and then the invitation to write without letting your hand stop moving for seven minutes. There is no space for wandering thoughts but also only space for wandering thoughts. The writing teeters between being utterly directionless and wholly focused. What comes out is poured purely from the well of our hearts and our grief. And it is most certainly prayer. Some call it journaling, or free writing, or guided reflection. I call it prayer. Even though it holds the most intimate sharing of what needs to be cried into words, we are asked to read it aloud to those in our break-out rooms. Knowing a piece will be shared or read to others almost always changes the way I write. But not here. If asked to lead prayers in a community, I always take the time to prepare. But not here.

Why is this so different? I think it is because I am lost in the experience of prayer, in a way that I would not be if I were praying out loud with a group, worrying about what was coming out of my mouth. The only difference seems to be that it comes through my hands, not my mouth. I am not stopping to think or compose. I am allowing myself to pray freely. But the fear of failure is removed. There are no expectations of style or type. No need for explanations or understanding. Just the expelled expression of my essence. The response of the group reinforces this. One by one we read our writings. And each person in the group in turn echoes words that resonated for them. No comments, just echoes. And the writer receives back their own words. A call and response where the response is the call. A responsive reading. A litany.

I hold such an aversion to prayers that are uttered out loud *extempore*. And again, I understand that this is a meaningful practice for many. But for some reason, if it is written spontaneously, as in Mirabai's practice, or sung, the directionless path of prayer feels completely different. There I crave the feeling of being lost in prayer.

I asked Hazzan Harold Messinger, cantor from a synagogue near me, to lead my Christian congregation in a session of Jewish chants. The first time he did so, he came with a pocketful of his regular chants and led us one by one through Hebrew words that were unknown to most of the people gathered. Several of his offerings were *niggunim*, wordless chants, where the melody itself is the prayer. Each chant lasted about five minutes. Beautiful. Hauntingly deep. Then at the end of our time together he mentioned that he might normally sing just one of those chants for twenty minutes at a time with his congregation. And my congregants said, 'Yes, that. That's what we want to experience too.' So the next time he came, he led us in twenty minutes of *Olam Chesed*

Yibaneh. Members of his congregation joined us, and some Muslim, Baha'i and Buddhist friends as well, all of us singing

> *Olam Chesed Yibaneh*
> *I will build this world from love*
> *And you must build this world from love*
> *And if we build this world from love*
> *Then God will build this world from love*[44]

Over and over we sang, eyes closed, time becoming meaningless. When the guitar strings stilled and the eyes flickered open, we looked around at one another, questioning. Had they also just been where I was? Harold recognized the look of wonderment in our faces, and explained – if we found ourselves lost at any point during that time, we were probably praying. Draped in words that we might not understand, lost in them, even in the prayers that aren't actually words, we are most deeply connected. This is prayer. The unknown and the unfamiliar perhaps heighten our powers of awareness and the depth of our connection. Connection to ourselves and to something beyond ourselves. It is not surprising during a time like this to feel a connection to those who are on the other side of the veil as well.

It seems as if being lost and being aware could stand in opposition. But perhaps they stand hand in hand. Lost in the bogs of a Hebridean island trying to find a marble quarry. Or lost in our direction in life as our career takes a sharp turn away from employment. Lost in a love that feeds and nurtures our wellbeing. Or lost in a relationship in which we no longer see ourselves. Lost in a wandering and delightful sort of way. Or lost in a directionless and disoriented sort of way. In whatever the circumstances, our awareness is attuned. The senses are awakened.

The Satipaṭṭhāna Sutta, the Buddhist Discourse on the Establishing of Mindfulness which stands at the core of vipassana meditation practice, teaches us to pull ourselves back from wandering thoughts. The monkey brain leads us to the suffering of our bodies, minds and hearts where we stand in our desires and dependencies. Through mindfulness practice we center ourselves in awareness in order to find liberation from suffering. I have often been victim of the monkey brain, especially at night when the mind swirls in the anxiety of feeling lost. I have found myself physically picking up my intangible thoughts with pinched fingers to pull them back to my center, to re-establish my awareness and mindful presence. And then, a few breaths later, to chase down those wandering thoughts and mind spirals as they skitter away again.

And now I practice being lost.

Whether they are going in circles or on a directionless path, my thoughts are taking me somewhere. So now I reframe them as prayer. A practice often disregarded in our age of mindfulness is that of distracted prayer. What are those things that pop in and occupy the space where sleep should be or that draw you away from a centered meditation? Follow them, with heightened awareness of the senses that are engaged. Where the body aches and the heart grips in your chest. Where the pulse starts pounding and the throat dries. Follow them and walk with them. Be lost in them. And perhaps if you find yourself lost, you are praying.

Our prayers come in the quietness of the guided meditation and in the windy roar of the muddy moor. And more often than not, they don't need words.

'Like a heavy sky that will never discontinue being filled with the weighty blessings of rain, the heart longs to open again to pour in a way that enlivens all the earth in its great, surrendered release of sorrow. And as the sunshine of remembrance spreads its wide, golden arms in your chest, it becomes clear again – The clouds, too, were God.'[45]

Chelan Harkin

Practice

LOVING WORDS

There was one Black singer in the church choir when I was growing up. Bailus Webb. A baritone with a voice that could reach down into your core and pull your heart out onto your lap. He was usually given a Negro spiritual to sing as a solo. And the staid Presbyterian congregants, unsure how to express their emotions, quietly wrestled with the depth of their feelings stirred by his heartfelt offerings. My father, who faithfully measured the rhythms of the liturgical year through the same annually repeated hymns and anthems, ensured that Bailus sang 'I Wonder as I Wander' every Christmas.

I wonder as I wander out under the sky
How Jesus, the savior, had come for to die
For poor on'ry people, like you and like I.
I wonder as I wander out under the sky.

A hymn made popular by John Jacob Niles who was said to have picked it up from a chant sung by a young girl in Appalachia. Four lines repeated. Perhaps he became lost in these words as we became lost in the Hebrew chants of Hazzan Harold. In the mountains, happening upon a young girl lost in thought and song. In Scotland, young children use the question 'How?' the way people in the States would use the word 'Why?' ('How is the sky blue?')

So when Bailus sang these lines, in a dark and stilled church sanctuary, I heard the wondering and wandering, I saw a darkened sky, and I understood the question, why had Jesus come to die. And why are we talking about him dying when it's Christmas? He just got here.

The wondering and wandering has stayed with me all these years. And the image of being lost in my questions out under the sky.

When I became more interested in language, I wanted those two words, wonder and wander, to be connected. Old English *wandrian* and *wundor* were not from the same Germanic root but further back, in fossils of our language, they both evolved from the Proto-Indo-European root *wen* which holds the idea of *striving* and *desiring*.

So as far as I am concerned, they both hold the notion of *praying*. And the understanding that praying is an act of wonder and wandering. And being lost. And being under the sky with questions so big that only the sky can hold them.

And perhaps something to look into more, if you are interested: a study by Tamara Embrey that links the Buddhist practice of the taming of the wandering mind from the Satipaṭṭhāna Sutta with Polyvagal Theory.[46]

RETHINK ...

the need for preparation and direction in prayer.

REFRAME ...

lost as the place where the possibilities become endless, where the senses are heightened and the awareness that lies within us and beyond us is keener.

REIMAGINE ...

releasing ourselves from the need for direction. We can allow our hearts to take us where they need to be, to sit in the presence of joy and pain, knowing that in whatever the circumstances, we are not alone. In the depth of loss perhaps comes the closest connection to that which is on the other side of the veil.

Chapter 14
Finding Direction

Practice
wilderness

Messengers

I have said that my sense of direction is defunct. I have recounted my boggy woes of not finding the marble quarry. I have learned that it is best for me to hand over the task of navigating. I haven't even mentioned that every time I step out of an elevator, I do not know which way to turn. Or that every year I arrived late with my children to my friend's Sunday School Easter party, because I couldn't tell the difference between the White Horse Pike and the Black Horse Pike. My dear friend Carol would be waiting for me, making sure I arrived. She thought that GPS devices were causing the decline in directional awareness for us as a civilization. A visual artist, she was particularly in tune with the markers that guided her through life. Everything held shape and color and perspective for her. Everything was potentially a signpost along the way. She was for me one of those messengers you encounter in life that have an internal compass, that you walk beside because you know they are going in the right direction.

    She was there the first time I found myself in the wilderness.

    My father was dying.

    I was twenty years old, traveling to my weekly Greek drama seminar in college, when I got the call from my mother that they were on their way to the hospital. It was a heart attack. Time went into slow motion. The ten days that he lived exist in some timeless capsule in my memory. A constant flow of church members visiting, weeping, needing care while they cared for us. People kept telling us that the best doctors in the city of Philadelphia were taking care of him, while I watched his legs turn black and wondered how he would stand in the pulpit again. He was not able to speak for most of those ten days, but after regaining stability following cardiac arrest, there was something he needed to tell us. There were messengers.

The impact of this statement cannot possibly be imagined unless you picture again a black-robed Scottish minister, born in the slums of 1920s Govan in Glasgow to a shipbuilder father from the docks of the Clyde. Yes, he was the man that talked to the cardinals in the dogwood tree beside his statue of the Buddha. But about near-death experiences of seeing things, not a chance. He called just the three of us, my mother, my brother and me, close so that only we could hear. There had been a light, and two messengers, and he told them he still had work to do.

What to do with this information? Was it a sign that he was to recover? He had pushed away the black-suited men I pictured who had come to get him. It was not his time, I was sure. How could I deny that he had been to the door of death and returned even though I knew this was not something he ever would have talked about or, dare I say, believed? And the urgency in telling us. Were we meant to share this news or were we called in close because it was just for us?

As the ten days brought increasing signs that his organs were dying, he did, in fact, have work that he continued to do, even hooked up to a million monitors and not able to move. There were messages for everyone who visited his bedside, scribbled on scraps of paper with a pen held upside down, its ink struggling to reach the ballpoint. And one last message that he managed to speak to me. It was about the way the nurses and doctors acted around him. 'If I don't make it out of here,' he whispered just to me, 'sue them for tragic faces.' My response: 'That's going to make a great sermon title one day, Dad.'

Then on the first Sunday of Lent, at exactly the time he would have been stepping into his pulpit, he followed those messengers. His work done.

There was no GPS for the wilderness of those days. My first experience with grief. But there were messengers. All around me. And Carol and her husband Peter became the markers for all the significant events of my life that were to come in the following years. My graduation, my marriage, the birth of my three children, my divorce, my journey through seminary to my own ministry. Peter held together the church that was reeling from the loss of a landmark. A young minister and new father himself. And I have no doubt in my mind that he was able to find his way because Carol shared her internal compass with him.

Whoever, whatever those messengers were that my father encountered, they were a part of his journey. As were those doctors with their tragic faces. My father used to scold doctors who set a time limit on people's lives with their diagnoses. And their faces were communicating the limit on his own life. Even at a time when he had dared to say 'not yet' to death.

In these times that mark our lives, defining moments, wilderness moments, I am convinced that there are messengers. Seen and unseen. We might be walking along a path to class and find ourselves veering into the woods. And there will be tragic faces that make us think there is no way out. But there will be ephemerals in the woods, and blazes, and the musky scent of a deer. There will be someone to tell you that you don't need to navigate just now because they will accompany you to the other side.

These messengers, they are leading you in prayer.

At the Distance of a Bowshot

It was decades later that I would step into the pulpit that my father never stepped into again. He also died two chapters into the book he was writing which was to be called *The Preparation of the Preacher*. I wondered if, along with suing those doctors for tragic faces, I might be meant to finish that book for him. After many years of asking myself if I should continue his work, so abruptly cut off at the age of sixty-five, I realized that I had my own path to follow. But I needed to head into that wilderness of ministry in order to find my path on the other side.

Ironically the part of that journey that I loved the most was the *preparation for preaching*.

The process of accompanying the text for a week or two and bringing it into a shared experience with a congregation became an act of prayer. It began with reading the text in many different translations and creating my own from the ancient languages that I loved so dearly. I walked with the text as it became part of my daily life and thoughts.

Finding Direction   153

My very breathing. Illustrations and connections encircling me like shades from the otherworld. Connections arising to events in my own life, the life of my community, the world, to larger theological themes. And then finding the words to make this prayer sound like a sermon.

As I came closer and closer to the days when a group of people would judge me worthy of being ordained, I found myself preparing to preach about Hagar from the book of Genesis. I began sitting with Hagar, at the distance of a bowshot. Driven out by Abraham, on Sarah's request, Hagar wandered in the wilderness.

> *So Abraham rose early in the morning, and took bread and a skin of water, and gave them to Hagar, putting them on her shoulder, and the child, and sent her away; and she went and wandered in the wilderness of Beer-sheba. When the water in the skin was finished, she cast the child under one of the bushes. And she went, and sat herself as far away opposite as one shoots a bow ...*[47]

Sarah demands that Abraham cast out this slave woman so that Ishmael will not inherit along with her son Isaac. This request does not sit easily with Abraham, but just as we are cringing at Sarah, God steps in and agrees with her. Double cringe. Abraham gave them bread and water. Then the water runs out. Hagar cannot take care of her son any more. So she casts him under a bush, and sits at the distance of a bowshot.

Hagar is in the wilderness. One can only imagine she has come to the point where she can't go on. She is depleted and destitute. What must it be like to leave your child under a bush? She sits at the distance that one can shoot an arrow from a bow. What an interesting image. But what is it meant to conjure? Was it a simple measure of distance? One translation says about a hundred yards. That was the phrase that inhabited me in my preparation. And also the sheer depletion of Hagar. The moment that she had nothing left to give.

Those moments can come to us at expected times, after a trauma, a loss, a diagnosis, a transition to a new stage of life that demands the entirety of our strength, physical, mental, emotional, spiritual. And at unexpected times, when you think you are handling everything just fine. For me it was at the end of my years of seminary. I had held down a full-time teaching position and seminary classes for five years. But in the final year, I wondered if I had found myself in the wilderness and cast my children under a bush.

The school year was coming to an end, the time that teachers and students (and I was both at the time) look to as the natural ordering of things. The time for rest, reflection and replenishing. But this summer would be different. I faced the hurdle of my clinical pastoral training in a hospital. The work of a chaplain in trauma care and hospice. Death every day. Room after room. There is nothing like a hospital chaplaincy to teach you how to pray. I have never prayed so much in my life. I spent so much time praying *with* and *for* others, that it really did not occur to me to pray *for* and *by* myself. The last thing I wanted to do was pray any more than I was.

I turned to a favorite passage from Julian of Norwich, feeling as if she could center me again in my relationship of personal prayer. Julian, the great Christian mystic of the 14th century. Living in the time of Chaucer, she was the first published female author to write in English, although she claimed to be unlettered. Julian was near death with the plague, had received last rites, and in the midst of her pain she questioned why there was sin in the world, believing sin was the cause of pain. She received a comforting vision of a Trinity that was not simply Father, Son and Holy Spirit, but male and female. Our maker, keeper, lover, joy and bliss.[48] A vision of a Christ who mothered in compassion, telling her that all would be well. Her vision became her prayer, as Jesus spoke to her, and she spoke back.

All will be well, and all will be well. All manner of thing will be well.

Julian was in relationship with her triune God, and God gave her what she needed, closeness, presence, relationship, an expansive view. This vision became her prayer in her time of wilderness.

I continued to sit with Hagar as well. Hagar who reached the point at which she had nothing left to give her child. Not an inheritance, not a home, and at the last not even any water. And she cast him under a bush – and sat at the distance of a bowshot. So why the bowshot? In the midst of my intensive seminary studies, I read it as a commentary on feeling separated from God. Or the sin that Julian had questioned. Sin as a matter of relationship, or rather the loss of relationship. Then I saw it. Hagar was keeping herself in relationship with God at that distance.

> She comes to the moment of having nothing left.
> Cast out. No water. No hope.
> BUT cries out: let me not look on the death of my child.
> She was praying.
> God opened her eyes and there it was.
> Water.
> Just what she needed
> Although God hears the boy, God doesn't save the boy.
> God saves Hagar.
> God shows the mother how to save her son.
> God showed her she had what she needed.

The secret of the bowshot lies in the Greek and Hebrew words for sin which are both rooted in terms about shooting a bow – missing the mark, a bullseye, being off center. Hagar is sitting at the distance of a bowshot. The appropriate distance to be able to hit the mark. She keeps herself in relationship with God. Although she is completely depleted, gives up, has no more, to the point that she leaves her son for death

> She cries out.
> And God hears.
> This is a dialogue.
> They are in relationship.
> They are outside the grip of sin.
> They are right on target.

It can't be a coincidence that this passage ends by saying that Ishmael grows up to be good at the bow. God makes of Ishmael a nation as well. Even though the promise is fulfilled through Isaac, the chosen line. Even though God tells Abraham that Sarah is right, cast her out. Hagar is not cast out of relationship. And Ishmael becomes the father of Islam. Our Muslim brothers and sisters are not cast out of relationship with us.

My Presbyterian studies were teaching me about being brought back into right relationship with God, but I realized I had some responsibility here. I had to stay as close as a bowshot, close enough not to miss the mark, and the way I needed to do that was to cry out into the wilderness, out of my depletion, and exhaustion, and failure. To cry out, even when I didn't have anything left to say, when I had no more praying left in me.

Just crying out.

Visceral. Deep. Primal.

A prayer that is nothing more than a sound, or one word, an image in the mind, one breath,

And a space to listen for God's presence.

All will be well. And all will be well. All manner of thing will be well.

Sitting with Wisdom

Sustaining for me was also the thought of my upcoming return to Iona. My yearly trek to the place that brings my body, breath and mind back into alignment. I was leading a group from my church that summer to stay on the island for a week, but I knew that I, as much as anyone else, needed the time for reflection on the year I had just finished.

The week was beautiful in every way, from glorious sunshine to seeing people that I cared about falling in love with the place I loved myself so dearly. And, as is often the case, witnessing people having transformative experiences in this thin place. I watched a childhood friend run up the hill that peaks the center of the island, Dun I. She carried with her the ashes of her father's body. Her mother stood beside me as we watched her ascend in a matter of minutes, disappear behind the top, and return, having found release for him, for them, for eternity. Another dear friend, having come to Iona in what she knew would be her final years with cancer, stood beside her own daughter and watched this scene unfold. She knew in this moment that her daughter would be able to go on after she died. She expressed that she was ready for what came next. Buoyed by the witness of this other young woman. Day after day, fellow travelers told me of the answers they were receiving to questions, the connections they were feeling, the space they had found to discern directions. Deeply, deeply moving experiences.

But it just wasn't happening for me. I wasn't getting my answers. I wasn't having my transformative experience. In a final gathering of the group, I assured the assembled that we do not always know in what way we have been transformed by an experience, and that we should keep our hearts open to the spirit which would continue to move and work within and through us as we moved on from this place. I was speaking to myself. I had wanted, I had needed, what they had received during that week. Some certainty about my final steps towards ministry.

The next day we stopped to tour in Edinburgh, and there I met her. Sofia. She was sitting on the street as people walked by, some chiding her for begging, for being in the way where tourists wanted to walk. I walked past her too. When I got back to my room, with an almond-crusted macaroon from the bakery in a greasy little brown paper bag, my treat for the night, I couldn't get her face out of my mind. I knew her. How did I know her?

Stuffing my macaroon back in my pocket, my hood up because it had started to rain, I went back out onto the street to find her. She wasn't where she had been ten minutes before, but I found her down another side street. She was huddled under layers and layers of clothing, faded from the colors they used to be. A cloth over her head. Her face soft with rivers of wrinkles. I handed her the little brown bag with a little bow of my head. And sheepishly walked back to my room.

I spent the night feeling foolish that for some reason I had thought a macaroon would be something useful to give this woman in the street, in the rain, in the night.

The next day, taking my group from the castle to the palace for a day of touring before our return to the States, there she was. Sitting on the steps of an old building, looking down at the ground and trying not to be seen. I gave an excuse to the group that I needed to use the bathroom, to go on without me, and I took a spot on the steps next to her. We just sat, next to one another, for a while. Then we started to speak. It was a language that was not hers nor mine, but some mingling of roots of words that made a conversation. I left for a few minutes to get us some lunch, and when I came back, a man was spitting on her. Telling her to go home. I took my spot again and tried to erase the sound of scorn that he had spewed on her. What we said, I have no idea. But I know we named and blessed each other's children. When I got up to leave, I asked for her name. Sofia. I had been sitting with Sofia. When I returned home, her face stayed with me. I knew it so well. And then one day it came to me. I remembered where I had seen her face before.

I was nine years old. I was carrying my favorite doll clothed in the red and white dress that my granny had knitted for her. It felt safe to hold on to her while we made our way through what seemed like the largest crowd of people I had ever encountered. My parents were holding on to me as tightly as I was holding on to Pebbles. We made our way as far as we could down the parkway sea of people until nothing more stood between us and the steps of the Art Museum but a police barricade. And there she was at the top. A slip of a woman bathed in a white robe with a blue stripe. A face with a river of wrinkles. She did not seem to be much bigger than my doll. I don't know what she said. I don't even remember hearing her voice. But I heard the hush of the massive crowd of people.

We waited while a limousine carried her away. We kept our place steady at the barricade, at the edge of the road, at the bottom of the steps. And then something happened that I will never forget as long as I live. The limousine stopped right in front of where I was standing, and she looked right at me and my doll and pressed her hand against the window. Her gaze lasted a lifetime. I still feel it. The prayer she made with a hand pressed against the glass and a look straight into my eyes was louder than any prayer I had heard before. In that moment I experienced the connection of the divine. I was utterly and completely embraced by an aura of love.

Two years later my father was instrumental in bringing Mother Teresa back to Philadelphia for the International Eucharistic Congress as the bicentennial was being celebrated in our city of sibling love. I stayed in Scotland with my mother while he made arrangements for Catholics and Protestants to be in communion through the washing of feet in circles of twelve, since the sharing of bread and wine or body and blood would not be a possibility. He took the occasion to tell

Mother Teresa how deeply moved I had been by her touch through the glass. She took a little scrap of paper, and wrote the words: *Margaret, Jesus loves you. Love others as he loves you.* I treasure this scrap of paper, for sure. But this written prayer holds nothing in comparison to the prayer we shared with our eyes.

But that was it! That was the face I saw in Sofia. Of course it was. I explained it away because there surely was a resemblance between two little old Balkan women.

Mother Teresa spent her life sitting with those who were outcast. People who put a biblical label on her witness say she was following Christ's directive as known from the Gospel of Matthew: whatever you do to the least of these, you do to me. But Mother Teresa had a most beautiful way of understanding this phrasing, *the least.* Every day she and the sisters in her order rose at 4:30 a.m. with the intent of finding the 'least of these' to whom they could minister. To ask her who were the least, 'Ek. Ek. Ek,' she would say, which in Hindi means 'One. One. One.' The least, we think of as the lowest, but to her the least meant the lowest number. Just one. Her encounters were with just one at a time.

One woman in a limousine, protected from a massive crowd of devotees. One woman spat upon by some and unnoticed by most. One woman nearing death from the plague with a vision of wellbeing. One woman casting her child under a bush and crying out in the wilderness. One woman with an internal compass pointing her towards beauty. One. One. One. And when you see her in one face, you recognize her in another.

They are my messengers.

The ones through whom I know I still have work to do.

Practice

LOVING WORDS

The world's traditions are replete with theophanies – the appearance of divine beings to humans, sometimes in human form themselves. Classical mythology is filled with wonderful stories of gods appearing in the guise of everything from cows to showers of golden rain to your best friend who lives down the street. In my Latin classroom I used this as the warning that comes to treat all people as if they might be a god in disguise. To the early Christians of Rome it was not an unusual thing for God to appear in human form. That's what gods did. To bring the messages they needed to bring. In the Hebrew scripture of Hagar in the wilderness, Cornelia Horn suggests, we are prepared for an appearance from God because of certain signs. Someone in a state of utter depletion and the mention of an empty vessel in a place known to have water prepares the reader's expectations for a theophany.[49]

And then there is this interesting verse. *But God heard the voice of the boy; and an angel of God called to Hagar from the heavens, and said to her: What's up with you, Hagar? Don't be afraid; because God has heard the voice of the boy from the place where he is.*[50]

Ishmael is not named anywhere in this text but is referred to repeatedly as 'the boy' or 'the son of Hagar'. But the first two words of this verse make up Ishmael's name: וַיִּשְׁמַע אֱלֹהִים (va-**yishma el**ohim), meaning 'God hears'. And that is exactly what happens in this verse. Hagar is not able to listen to the cries of the boy, thinking that he is at the point of death. God responds directly to the boy, but an angel of God is the one to respond to Hagar.

Angels are messengers. An angel, ἄγγελος (angelos), brings a message, ἀγγελία (angelia). And although we understand Hagar to have received a message from God, it is important to remember that these divine messages come from those who meet us in the place where we are. So careful, lest you are not aware that you are entertaining angels.

RETHINK ...

where we look for direction in the wilderness – for it often appears in the most unexpected places.

REFRAME ...

the understanding of wilderness as the time and space of emptying. It may come from depletion and exhaustion, from standing at the door of death, from not knowing what is next, but in that wilderness, may we be open to those that come in visions and on the street, to put us in direct connection with the divine.

REIMAGINE

Dignity comes not just because, as some understand, we were created in the image of God, but just as surely because God became the image of us.

Chapter 15
Taking a New Path

Practice
the impulse and the imperative
to pilgrimage

Chrysalis Soup

The labyrinth started to breathe. As those gathered for a sunset walk made their way into the center, into circles expanding and contracting, it became the very image of a pulsing heart. The crunching of measured footfalls, step after slowed step, sounded the beats. Walkers fell into rhythm, on a journey alone but as part of a living, breathing organism. A chrysalis.

The Outdoor Chaplain, Rev. Cairn Neely, was our labyrinth walk guide. He described the meditative practice of walking into the labyrinth as resembling the wrapping of the chrysalis, enveloped in possibility. The reflective act of walking out of the labyrinth resembled the release of the chrysalis, renewed in transformation. Wrapped in the layers of this experience, the walkers were witness to the changes happening within and beyond themselves.

This particular labyrinth was the vision and creation of Rev. John Woodcock, labyrinth leader and long-time pastor of the Church of the Loving Shepherd. Woodcock has been an advocate of interfaith engagement for his more than 50-year ministry. His life's work centered on creating a sanctuary from a converted barn on a property named Bournelyf. The site is a sanctuary for those seeking communion with spirit, regardless of the way in which they find its center. It is home to an ecumenical Christian congregation, a Buddhist sangha, and launched the Jewish community of Beth Chaim. Chaim, the Hebrew word for life, the very life that flows from Bournelyf, the Stream of Life. The labyrinth was wrapped into the landscape, enveloping the trees and melting into the folds that roll towards the stream. And during the Chrysalis walk, it began to breathe.

The Outdoor Chaplain gathered the walkers before we began our contemplative practice, encouraging us to still our thoughts, our pace, our breath. Rather than giving instructions, he modeled a close attunement with the creation into which we were stepping. He was already in conversation with the land around us, with the labyrinth itself. He walked it before everyone else arrived, letting it know of our plan. Asking it for guidance. Sharing in its conversation. Belden Lane, theologian and professor of environmentally-centered spirituality and author of *The Great Conversation* writes:

> *We're surrounded by a world that talks, but we don't listen. We're part of a community engaged in a vast conversation, but we deny our role in it ... The Earth yearns to teach us languages we didn't even know existed.*[51]

Neely listens. Neely is already part of the conversation. And he welcomes the labyrinth walkers into it too. He shared an image with the group. In its metamorphosis from caterpillar to butterfly, the pupa in its chrysalis stage becomes soup. A soup of proteins that reorganize into the beings that they are to become. He encouraged us not to focus on any transformation we might hope for, any expectations that we might hold, but just to become the soup. It was astounding how quickly the dissolving happened. The power of the labyrinth pulls you into its whispered conversation where expectations dissolve. With every footstep landing only in front of the last one, there is no way of telling how far into the journey you are. Concentric circles take you close to the middle and then out to the edge again and again, with no hint of measuring the path. Soup. A golden soup, as the name chrysalis takes from the Greek. Pure. Present. Pulsing.

When we landed in the center, all having walked our own path with our own thoughts and our weights dissolving, we stopped there. Unplanned and unexplained, we craved that moment of connection in the middle. Not to speak or even look at each other, but just to breathe together for a few minutes before one by one we headed back out. Proteins aligning.

As we unwound, each releasing our chrysalis, the sun was dipping below the horizon, shedding its golden glow. Our faces lifted to the west for its blessing, each time we rounded in that direction. Gold met gold. Neely had shared with us before we embarked the Indigenous Prayer to the Four Directions from Chief Si'ahl. Calling spirit into each direction that we faced as we walked the labyrinth that mirrored creation, we exited to the west.

> *Great Life-Giving Spirit, I face the West (black), the direction of sundown. Let me remember every day that the moment will come when my sun will go down. Never let me forget that I must fade into you. Give me a beautiful color, give me a great sky for setting, so that when it is my time to meet you, I can come with glory.*[52]

The silence of the conversation was rich with shared experience. A fox stood at a distance and nobody needed to point to it or exclaim that there was a fox to which we should all turn. We were all now in conversation without words. We were part of a community engaged in a vast conversation. And we were listening. As we parted, Neely shared his experience of watching us engaged in the walk, individuals on our own journeys of transformative practice. We were the breath that made the labyrinth expand and contract. The labyrinth became a beating heart, the lungs of the earth, the teacher of a language we didn't even know existed. A prayer we did not know we were praying.

Companions on the Journey

Belden Lane, Christian mystic writer of our times, the one who had the chancel view of my father kneeling before preaching, and, as he describes himself, a recovering scholar, takes to the wilderness 'with John Ruysbroeck or Hildegard of Bingen, now and then with Rumi or Lao-tzu.'[53] I myself travel with Belden Lane in my backpack. His breadth of experience, his filing-cabinet-mind-ful of references and stories, his ability to take us into the wilderness with him and to see ourselves in his learnings make me feel at once that I should not ever attempt to put pen to paper, and at the same time that it is the only thing I should be doing.

On one of my annual trips to Iona a few years ago, his latest book,

The Great Conversation: Nature and the Care of the Soul, was going to be my companion text for the time I was there. Cooried into my wee room after the first evening of prayers in the abbey, I took out my companion to savor some pages before the shadow of a traveler's sleep descended. The first paragraph finds Belden taking the dirt road toward the monastery at Ghost Ranch in New Mexico. My journey mirrored his, although by ferry, to my monastic destination. The pages turned, the sleep did not come, and then the overwhelming need to close the book at page 57.

> *Pilgrimage is a spiritual as well as biological impulse, cutting across species.*[54]

He writes about the instinct for migration, the impulse to pilgrimage, in cranes and wildebeests and caribou and butterflies and terns, and humans on the Camino de Santiago, and journeying to Mecca, and the Earth itself on its path around the sun. I couldn't read another word. It was everything. I didn't read any more on my entire journey. I didn't finish this beloved treasure of a book until months after I returned. I couldn't. This one line had filled up all the spaces in my mind and body. I set my companion aside, and I sank into what I knew was the deepest instinct and impulse in my spirit and body: to make this pilgrimage. How many times in my life had I made this journey, with my parents, then with my own children, with groups I was leading, with friends and colleagues. But it was not until I came by myself and even cast my companion of a book aside, that I was able to confront the wilderness of the journey.

In a previous book, *Backpacking with the Saints: Wilderness Hiking as Spiritual Practice,* Belden explains that wilderness is confronting whatever growth is imperative but also threatening in your experience. That wilderness involves risk but also a discipline.[55] The combination of imperative, impulse and instinct pulled me across the ocean, even though I was going to need to travel alone. And get on the right trains. Which I didn't. But I learned. And I kept going. I got lost. I kept going. I had made this journey fifty times. But never alone. And now I know it was something biological and spiritual. I had to go alone. For the growth that was imperative but also threatening in my experience.

Alone, but enveloped by a community of wild geese who taught me how to fly in a V formation.

The Wild Geese

The beautiful white dove is symbolic of peace, protection and purity in Judaism, Christianity and Islam. The harbinger of hope in Native American tradition. Columba. The dove that shares its name with the man who sailed his coracle to the forested beach at the south side of the island. The Holy Spirit itself.

It has nothing on the honking wild goose. 'The wild goose is not particularly elegant: its sudden honking overhead can pierce many a moment of quiet contemplation,' shares Annaliese Johnston, a volunteer from Aotearoa New Zealand, in a reflection in the abbey. Columba may take the name of the dove, but the Iona Community very aptly uses the wild goose as its guiding symbol.

One of the most beautiful things about living in community in the abbey is that it is almost always all hands on deck. Each person has their assigned job – housekeeping, sacristy, kitchen, administration; mine was working in the shop, as I've mentioned. But everyone helps everywhere, all day, doing what is needed. One of my favorite moments was when I was leading a group of new guests to the abbey through the routine of cleaning the toilets and showers one Sunday morning. Red gloves for the toilets, blue for the sinks and showers. I left them to it while I went to help set up communion for the service. I delivered the reflection in worship that morning, and then after a brief post-worship dance in the cloisters, I made my way to the shop where visitors and guests to the island were buying up their store of Fair Trade chocolate for the week and the books that would be their companions when they cozied in their rooms at night. A woman came up to the counter to buy a pair of our favorite wrist-warmers, and she said, 'Wait, wasn't I cleaning toilets with you this morning?' Yes, she was. 'Wait, did you just offer the reflection in the service?' I felt as if I was in an episode of *Fawlty Towers* for a moment, but the delight wafted over me. I was part of the V formation.

We each take turns leading the prayers in the morning and at night, pulling to the front of the V for some moments as we cup our wings together and honk our way through the tasks of the day. Praying for justice and peace, for healing, for universal love, for a sense of commitment that will carry beyond the ancient walls and over the Sound of Mull. Annaliese stood behind the leader's desk one evening, and she called us into community as the honking wild geese. Reminding us that sometimes we fall out of the V, in order to care for others. Or to allow others to care for us. Sometimes we have to stop battling the headwinds and let someone else take the lead. Sometimes we have to nestle down in the fields and regroup, regather, regird. But the beckoning honk, inelegant and disruptive as it may be, calls us to new adventures and courage, towards challenge, to changing direction, and to risk. To flapping around for a while in the process of finding our way.

Annaliese's words found me as I was coming to understand my spiritual and biological impulse to pilgrimage. As my chrysalis was becoming soup.

We are pulled into the wilderness. And whether we make the journey alone or in formation, there are guides who will take the lead. They don't need to be clergy. There are readings that will nourish. They don't need to be scripture. There are markers on the path. They might not be signposts. There are birds – not gentle doves, but flapping geese – honking their encouragement that the wild spirit is disruptive and risky but calls us to the growth that is imperative.

Practice

LOVING WORDS

Columba landed on the shores of Iona, where the Gaelic and Pictish peoples already knew the sacredness of this place – where sea, sky and stone seemed to meld in divine harmony. The name Columba, meaning 'dove', would come to symbolize peace and spiritual presence.

Centuries later, another figure bearing a similar name, Columbus, would land on distant shores with a different legacy – a legacy marked by the displacement and erasure of Indigenous peoples who also understood the sacredness of their lands, where birds, plants and the earth itself were kin.

The contrast is stark. The white dove descending as the Holy Spirit stands in tension with the honking brown goose, long a symbol of the Spirit for the Celtic tradition – a wild and earthy presence, loud and uncontainable. The dove – *columba* – entered Christian symbolism through Latin roots, from *kolomos* and further back to the Proto-Indo-European *kel-* meaning 'to cover, conceal, or protect'. These associations, though poetic, have at times been co-opted to justify colonial narratives of 'protection' and 'civilization', masking harm with a veneer of sanctity.

The goose, on the other hand, takes its name from the supposed sound of its honk.

Patty Krawec in her book *Becoming Kin* says, 'Being a settler or a colonizer is not something you are; it is something you do. It describes your relationship to this land and the people in it. Remember that settlers come to impose a way of living on top of the existing people. Settler colonialism destroys in order to replace. If you are going to stop being a settler and start being kin, that's where we start. With what you do.'[56]

Flying in V formation.

RETHINK ...

paths as leading forward only and direction as linear.

REFRAME ...

The understanding of pilgrimage as a journey into wilderness, where the destination is not nearly as important as the homecoming.

REIMAGINE ...

listening to our spiritual and biological impulse to take the risks that will call us to the growth that is imperative but also threatening to our experience. To recognize wilderness in taking the lead position of the V, forging into the headwinds, and also as flapping away from the V, to find if the path ahead is the one where we will find community.

Part Five

Practice Nourishment

Chapter 16

Sharing Sustenance

Practice
filling your cup
with what you want to spill out

Putting the Kettle On

My granny's words are the first thing that come to mind when any news is shared: *I'll put the kettle on*. From the greatest tragedy to the most sincere joy, the first step is the making of the tea. Living the village life, the knock at the door was a regular occurrence. A neighbor whose husband had been drinking the night before. The baby that wasn't going to make it home from the hospital. The minister come to visit. A long-awaited letter arrived by post from overseas with news of the immigrant couple settling in. I'll put the kettle on, was her response. Deaths, births, divorce, it was the first expression of 'I am in this with you. You are not alone. I will share it with you. Whatever it is.' No phrase has ever felt more nourishing to me. No communal prayer more connected.

When our parents died, my brother and I found some odd sort of bereaved amusement in counting how many times someone's response was, 'I'm sorry for your loss.' Words that I have warned future chaplains never to use. They are words that build a separation between the one expressing sympathy and the one who is grieving – your loss. Ick. How much more nourishing are the words 'I'll put the kettle on'? To this day the sound of water pouring from the kettle and tea flowing from the teapot cause me to take a deeper breath. The sound of being filled.

Secondary to the tea is the fact that you rarely have just a cup of tea in Scotland without a bite of something baked to accompany it. A scone, a piece of shortbread or, as my granny would say, just a wee biscuit. She did not understand my dabbling in different types of tea as I opened my cupboard to offer a choice of Earl Grey, Darjeeling, peppermint or green. My Iona workmate could not accept my taste for rooibos tea, calling it rubbish tea. The preference is for just *tea* tea. Because, I'm convinced, it's not really about the tea. It's about what happens over tea. It's about that expression 'I'll put the kettle on'.

I once had a student who was a deeply sensitive soul. He would bound into Latin class like a puppy, louder than anyone in the room. He would cry if he got a C on a quiz and tell me how angry his parents would be about the grade. One day he came to school in a right royal funk. Nothing was going right. I couldn't reason with him. I didn't need to solve his problem. I said, 'I'll put the kettle on.' I always had a kettle in my classroom and a cup for every one of my students. Sometimes sitting with a cup of tea was just more important than conjugating verbs. And sometimes conjugating verbs was much more manageable with a cup of tea by one's side.

That year when it was my birthday, I walked into my classroom and that student greeted me at the door: 'I've put the kettle on.' If he didn't remember a thing about Latin, I would not have cared. He had learned the beauty of human connection, of compassion, communicated over a cup of tea.

Filling Our Cups

I recall that riddle from my preaching professor, Karen Wiseman, about the spilled cup. In moments when life shakes us, whatever is inside us comes spilling out. We can fake our reactions some of the time, but when life crashes into us, what spills out is what is deeply held within the vessel of our beings. Cultivating a practice of prayer means filling our cups with what we would like to spill out, over our laps, our friends' shoulders, our co-workers and partners. I have a dear friend who makes beautiful videos for a YouTube channel she calls Cozy Contemplation. Videos of her walking in the woods and the snow. Noticing nature and being in the still and wild places around her. Every video concludes with her filling a cup with hot cocoa and sitting with it cradled in her hands. Her life of prayer. She takes her inspiration from Henri Nouwen's little treasure, *Can You Drink the Cup?*

> *We have to live our life, not someone else's. We have to hold our own cup. We have to dare to say: 'This is my life, the life that is given to me, and it is this life that I have to live, as well as I can.'*[57]

When she is struggling, she takes to the trail, and comes home to her kettle, a spoonful of ethically sourced cocoa, which she has carefully researched, knowing that it is from a single source. A dash of salt and vanilla. Some sugar and almond milk. When I am struggling, she sends me a reminder to go make myself a cup of hot cocoa. And she sends me a picture of her hands cupped around her own cup. Miles apart but sharing in prayer via text and cup. When life bumps into her, what comes spilling out is not hot cocoa, but compassion from the ways she has nourished her own wellbeing.

So we live our own lives, as Henri Nouwen says. We hold our own cup. And we fill it with practices that nourish and sustain us. As Belden Lane suggests, these are practices that hold discipline and also risk. The intention would be to fill that cup so that when something comes crashing into us, what spills out is the sustenance that filled it. A blend of compassion and self-love. But perhaps the reality is that when something crashes into us, we may just need to cry out with the frustration, anger and hurt that the collision has caused. So maybe we can reframe the filled cup.

We take to the trail to walk, we find connections to earth and to friends, we seek stillness, engage creativity, understand a million different ways to engage our hearts and minds in practice that nourishes. We understand them as practices of prayer. Not petition but presence. We come to understand the divine that resides within us, around us, and beyond us. Our cup is filling. And when we are jostled, our cup bursts with an explosion of life. Every part of it. The sorrow and the pain. The joy and the frustration. What spills out is our lives, ready to share and be shared, connected, seen, heard, known. And the crying out may be in petition or in lament. But at its core, it is the expression that everything we have poured into the cup of our lives holds us during these times. So cry, weep, scream, rage, and laugh too. It is all heard and held. And the tears water the land that grows the cacao bush that is harvested by the farmer, that your cup may be filled.

Drinking Water

We are vessels of water. The make-up of our bodies, our brains, our beings, is water. Studies from the National Institutes of Health find that our intake of water goes far beyond supporting the functioning of our physical systems. Adequate hydration lowers our risk of developing chronic diseases.[58] Beyond alleviating headaches, water intake mitigates depression and anxiety. All in balance, of course. Too much water and we mess with our sodium levels and can just as easily end up in the hospital for over-hydration as dehydration. Every day then offers the practice of taking in what we need. Water is necessary for our health and mental wellbeing. But is it not also a key component of our spiritual wellbeing? Explore the sacred texts of any tradition, and it is easy to find water as a basic element not just of life but of divine being. But perhaps these texts are also leading us to a spiritual practice. Our daily intake of water for physical and mental health is also an act of daily prayer.

Since my earliest years, I have been fascinated with the idea of flowing water. I could never pass a stream without begging my parents to stop the car and let me dip my hands in, even for a minute. In college I found Heraclitus, the pre-Socratic philosopher, and his philosophy of πάντα ῥεῖ (*panta rei*, everything flows) and the notion that one can never step into the same river twice. The image of the river, never static, always new to each person who steps in it, became symbolic for me of the need to flow. Through difficult times of life-transition, I have relied on the river for comfort, viewing life as the waters that must flow and not stand. Rabbi Toba Spitzer says, 'If we think of God as a mighty river flowing in the direction of justice and love, then one key component of spiritual practice is that we put ourselves in alignment with that flow.'[59]

Be the water.

A note found on a friend's Instagram post. It was advice from her therapist as she approached the impending holidays feeling anxious about impending tensions.

Be the water.

The image of flowing water, the touch of flowing water, the sound, the symbolism.

Water is an essential element of our wellbeing.

The beloved Psalm 23 of David in the Hebrew scriptures speaks of the Lord as a shepherd. He leads me besides still waters. And what happens as I lie in pastures green, beside those waters? Are they flowing, though gently enough to seem still? More likely this is a poetic device called a *transferred epithet*. I am the one who is still, not the water. Here I find the place where my soul is restored (יְשׁוֹבֵב), literally returned to me. I come back to a place of wholeness. In right relationship with my being and in my relationship with the divine. I find the source of all being in the water, as the water.

The verdant image of this scene, however, poses another possibility for my contemplative practice. As the sheep led to water, I am invited to drink. My life literally returned to me through the intake of the water, stilled for me to sip. A reminder that the act of picking up my water bottle can become part of my daily spiritual practice.

From Christian baptism to Islamic *wudu* ablutions, from Jewish *mikveh* to the Indigenous *Nahuatl* ceremony, water is central to our sacred rituals, both in community and in individual prayer. As we learn in Hindu tradition, water is the source of all being, the essence of life, and that to which we must return in death. The Upanishads tell us that our prana, our vital energy, comes from water (VI.5.1). Similarly in Muslim and Daoist traditions, water is not just an element of sacred ritual but is commensurate with the divine itself. In Quranic teaching, water is the epiphany of the divine qualities (al-asmā waṣ-ṣifāt).[60] In Daoism water is the essence-spirit (jing 精) and its downward flow brings celestial consciousness to all beings.

We are vessels of water. And we are vessels of the divine. Flowing around us and through us. Swelling our beings with life.

So as I consider my daily practices of prayer and meditation, whether that is daily reading of sacred texts, moments spent in prayer, unrolling my yoga mat, or taking a walk in nature, I intend to remember how vital the interaction with water is. Yes, the flowing river running through my fingertips in prayer. But also the water bottle that tags along for adequate hydration could just become the central focus of my contemplative practice. It is the water that flows within me that I am focusing on now.

Hydrating me.
Restoring my soul.
No need to gulp.
I mindfully let the water enter my body.
Feel it surround every organ that is working to sustain my living

and my thinking.
Feel it reach to the very bottom of the soles of my feet,
where I connect to the earth.
Where the water itself returns to the sky
to rain its celestial life force on me.
Be the water.
A vessel for the divine life source.

'You are water, whirling water,
Yet still water trapped within,
Come, submerge yourself within us,
We who are the flowing stream.'[61]
    Rumi

Baking Bread

As by now you have come to see, I have spent much of my time reframing my own understanding of prayer. Rethinking my expectations. Reimagining the ways in which I am in communication with divine presence. Hoping that somewhere along the way, someone who has been cast down by an experience of prayer that doesn't work or a tradition that does not feel nourishing might feel a sense of connection. And the experience of writing this has been a daily spiritual practice for me as well. I walk then I write. I put the kettle on then I write. I stretch my body then I write. I look out at the sea then I write. But more often than not, I approach my laptop with a dusting of flour somewhere on my sleeve or my cheek, a little bit of crusting dough on the side of my hand. Because the place in which I find my deepest practice of embodied prayer is with the heel of my hand pushing away and up, my fingers gathering, folding, turning, shaping, lost in the rhythm of creating nourishment.

I revisit with you the Saturday morning sacred space of sabbath of my childhood. The day when the sermon was prepared, the work set aside, when we, as a family, were in prayer together. Perhaps there are families out there who sit and say prayers together. Not us. Not by a long shot. Not in times of national disaster or family upheaval. We did not bow our heads together and pray. At dinner time, we uttered the same words every night, unthinkingly. No, we did not say prayers together. But we lived in prayer together. We lived in a yeasty, cheesy, soupy prayer together. After my mother and I lazed our way through the Saturday morning cartoons and breakfast in bed, we checked on my dad who would be at the first punching down of the rising bread. It's the only part of his physical being that I can still see with great clarity, the knuckles of his hands kneading, a Celtic cross ring on the finger of one hand and a square ring with his initials on the other. With the same concentration that he held when preparing on Sunday mornings, he worked the dough with a rhythm that spoke of drumming, the echo of which I still hear.

My mother stewed the ham hock for as many hours as the bread rose. And just before the lentils went in the pot and the shaped loaves went in the oven, we went as a family to the cheese shop to pick out the most pungent, creamiest, crumbliest, bluest choices of the week. My favorites were Appenzeller and Port Salut. I only learned as an adult that Port Salut, with its bright orange rind, was developed by Trappist monks in the Loire Valley. Undoubtedly their own spiritual practice, stirring the curds. We sat on those sabbath afternoons with soup and bread and cheese at our green metal table with its green vinyl chairs, and all was well, and all manner of thing was well.

I know it has surprised some of my friends over the years to think that the family of this powerhouse of the Presbyterian pulpit did not engage in seemingly 'religious' practices at home. We didn't read the Bible. We read Wordsworth and Burns. We didn't bow our heads in prayer. We took walks and named the trees. We whistled to the cardinals. We dug our hands into the soil and pulled out potatoes. And we shared a loaf of homemade bread on the sabbath, a pot of soup, and a hunk of cheese, named and chosen by each one around the table. This was our life of prayer. The source of our physical and spiritual nourishment. That which allowed us to know the presence of the divine within our warmed frames, in the valuing of the time we shared, and in the wonders that the earth had provided for our sustenance.

The Bread of Life

Biblical readings were not for storytelling in my upbringing. They were for questioning. Interpreting. Finding meaning and connection. Perhaps not surprising then that I was drawn to wonder about the words put in the mouth of Jesus of Nazareth in the Gospel of John. I am the bread of life. I am the bread that comes down from heaven. I am the living bread.

It is a statement of nourishment and wellbeing, of wholeness, one in which Christians ground a life of faith with an understanding that, as followers of Christ, we center our lives on a right way of living. Jesus is our nourishment. Jesus, however, built his teaching on metaphor, on parables. His very style of teaching sets us up to use him as an example. So perhaps in this statement Jesus is modeling something important for us. How do we fill our cups?

In the sixth chapter of the Gospel of John, the peers of Jesus, the people who have grown up with him, began to complain about him because he said, 'I am the bread that came down from heaven.' Who does he think he is, this guy from down the block? And how does Jesus respond? 'I am the bread of life,' he says again. He has chosen how he is going to identify himself, and in strength he does not let the complaints alter that.

I am the bread of life.

We have seen Jesus at this height of his ministry retreating, withdrawing up the mountain, over to the other side of the sea, for a moment to breathe, for some respite. After all of the scenes involving bread, feeding the crowds and teaching about the manna from heaven, Jesus lands here: I am the bread of life. He has filled his cup with this understanding, this assurance. And when the crowds come needing and thronging and complaining, what spills out of his cup is simply this. I am the bread of life. I am enough.

So what I'm suggesting is this. Is Jesus perhaps modeling for us how to fill our cups? Is this perhaps not so much about the metaphor, the well-worn and deeply analyzed metaphor that we must turn to Christ alone for salvation, but rather a modeling for us of connection to oneself.

I am enough
I am in connection with myself and with the divine
The divine that is within me
And the divine that is me
I am enough
I am the bread of life

We can understand this not simply as the imperative to get some of this living bread, but that we can be this bread. We are the bread of life. Jesus taught so much more than the need to profess faith in him, that we should nourish ourselves on the bread that is him. He modeled for us how to be like him. How to fill our cups, so when someone knocks into us, this is what will spill out.

Breaking Bread

I started to get anxious when there was no yeast left on the grocery store shelves. I had been to three stores. Sharing my panic that I would not be able to bake fresh bread in the isolation of pandemic, I received a message from a friend who had a sourdough starter. I could pick up a jar from her mailbox when she divided her starter the next day.

At this time when we were just learning how to be in community via Zoom, I desperately needed to knead. Maintaining this level of spiritual practice was going to be essential. So I joined the millions of people who fed their new sourdough practice daily.

Long before I decided to follow my father's footsteps into ministry, I had taken up his weekly practice of making bread for my children, for my friends, for anyone who stopped by to sit at table with us. But sourdough was new for me. A friend taught me the Hamotzi, the Jewish blessing of the bread

בָּרוּךְ אַתָּה, יְיָ אֱלֹהֵינוּ, מֶלֶךְ הָעוֹלָם הַמּוֹצִיא לֶחֶם מִן הָאָרֶץ

Baruch atah, Adonai Eloheinu melech haolam, hamotzi lechem min haaretz

Blessed are You, Lord our G-d, King of the universe, who brings forth bread from the earth

Into my first sourdough loaf, I kneaded gratitude for my friend who shared her starter, for the connection, for my children quarantined with me who would share this loaf, for those with whom I could not share this loaf but with whom I would connect in the new world of virtual classrooms and worship services. The loaf rose with my concern for those without bread that day, for those without connection.

Holy Week approached in these first weeks of lockdown, and I anticipated the loss of the familiar setting of my favorite service of the church year, Maundy Thursday. A service that is literally about communion with others, the celebration of the last supper of Jesus, when he broke bread at table with his disciples, in preparation for passing his ministry on to them, that they would find ways to connect with people as he had. What would it be like to celebrate by breaking bread at the table when the table was not there, when we couldn't pass the loaf to one another?

But then the most beautiful thing happened. One of the young people in my congregation had become a baker as well. I offered to share my starter with her, and her mom drove her over to pick up the jar from my mailbox. Then the idea – what if we passed this starter around our congregation? Could we strengthen our connection by sharing of the same bread? Members of the congregation left loaves on one another's doorsteps. For the ambitious, mason jars of starter were left with a sheet of instructions about how to tend to it daily. When Maundy Thursday came, the screen was filled with all the members of the congregation holding up a loaf that we might break bread together. And every loaf was from the same source. From the same bit of starter shared by my friend.

I do not know where the descendants of that starter are now, but I like to think of the journey it took from our congregation to another, poured into jars, left in mailboxes and on doorsteps, from one faith tradition to another. Some added seeds and nuts, some cut fancy designs into the skin, some sliced it with cheese, and some broke it apart with jam and butter. An expression of the manifold ways in which we embody nourishment and practice prayer.

Practice

LOVING WORDS

My children always knew when we were having company, because there would be napkins on the table, a luxury in which we did not usually indulge. In fact, they would tell some visitors that they must be on the 'one-of-the-family' list if there were not napkins laid out for their use. But another sure sign was bread rising on the counter. *Company* – those with whom (*com-*) we share bread (*panis*). When we find a *companion* to *accompany* us on our way, there is the expectation of shared nourishment. Sustenance through connection and communion. Some mistakenly associate the word 'union' with communion, overlooking the richness of its root, *munus*. Communion is the act of coming together (*com-*) to share our *munera* (gifts) with one another. In this understanding we can focus on the fact that we all bring different gifts to the table. We are not the same. Our traditions are not the same. They may not even have similar destinations, but in *communion*, we bring who we are, and what we have been given, in order to create *community* and find nourishment in one another.

RETHINK ...

prayer as an act of nourishment and sustenance found in community.

REFRAME ...

the ways in which we share sustenance with another as a deep act of love. The earth gives us seed which we grow and harvest, dry and grind, knead and leave to rise. In the pouring of a cup of tea and the breaking of bread, we are in communion with the earth and our neighbor.

REIMAGINE ...

being taught that care and compassion and generosity and gratitude and sorrow and solidarity could all be conveyed with the simple prayer of presence. And a boiling kettle.

Chapter 17

Embracing Creativity

*Practice
creating with no judgement
for the process not the product*

The Scent of Creation

The smell of oil paints and turpentine activates a deep sense of calm for me. All is well. The bread is rising, the soup is on, and my father is on the third floor of the manse in his painting space. Curiously creeping into the room, I am invited into the naming of the colors that will scrape onto the palette that morning. Cadmium yellow, cerulean blue, titanium white, burnt sienna. The pictures hang on my walls around me now, castles and lochs, mountains and temples, each a prayer painted by my father in his sabbath moments of embracing creativity.

    Brian McLaren reminds us that everything that we call human culture, from music to science, and art to engineering, is an act of creativity. 'Created not by God, but by humans, who, as image-bearers of the Creator, are themselves creative.'[62] Connecting ourselves to our creativity is one of the most profound ways of merging with the source of life, the power of creation, the divine presence, God the Creator. Sharing our creativity connects us to the divine that *is* our relationship with one another. Seeking new forms of creative expression opens us to the divine in the wonders and mystery of all creation.

    Perhaps you, like me, can name all the creative gifts you wish you had been given. Oh, that my fingers could glide across the piano keys and my voice produce more than a thin wafer of a song. That I could capture the birds outside my window with those colors on the palette. It was my friend Carol who taught me that I was devaluing the creative gifts I had by not recognizing them. She taught me to see that I am an artist, even though I cannot draw a stick figure. I will never forget one day when she was giving her full presence to my son, her godson, out on our back deck. There was a puddle from the previous night's rainfall, and my two-year-old was heading for it. I reached to lift him away from getting his pants wet. She reached to take his hand and press it into the puddle. Then onto the dry deck. Then back into the puddle. Handprints formed an ephemeral flower pattern on the wooden slats. Gone in a few minutes, but a simple prayer shared by the two of them. She embraced the moment that brought connection between two loved ones, the beauty of the Earth, and the gift of creativity.

The Shape of Creation

Sondra Rosenberg, who created the beautiful painting for the cover of this book from a photograph of one of my favorite spots on Iona, is an artist and art therapist who is deeply connected to the gifts of the Earth. She has spent many years providing art therapy to people with eating disorders as well as offering creative workshops for personal exploration and healing. She led a workshop for participants in an Alignment retreat in which she introduced us to the spirit-nourishing journey of independent and collaborative artmaking, inspired by the work of Andy Goldsworthy, a British land artist whose outdoor sculptures made from natural materials stand until the wind blows or a wave washes them away. Sondra walked us into the woods where she left us to create our own installations. Twigs and vines were twisted. Rocks set in patterns on the path. Creations hanging from trees, encircling trees, climbing trees. Each one a prayer in the making and the sharing. As Belden Lane says, each person was 'recognizing a wisdom and creativity that comes through them, but also from beyond them – from the earth itself.'[63] She reminds each one present that we must never judge our acts of creation or fear that they are not good enough. Each one is enough. Each one is an act of beauty.

My phone pings with a message, a WhatsApp voice recording of a Latvian prayer, sung gently in the night through pain and sorrow, by my friend Urzula Glienecke. And a picture of a sculpture she made from translucent resin. Water splashing into the dark. A cry of release. The embodiment of liberation from captivity. An ode to fragility and resilience. And a poem that accompanies the form, *When the Dark Closes In*.

> Sometimes the dark seems
> To close up
> Around us
> Above us
> Beneath us
> Within us
> The world situation
> Cruel deeds
> Hurtful words
> Or just ... life
> But at the very heart of the dark
> There
> Is
> A Presence
> A blessing
> A loving touch
> A compassion to carry us through
> We are not alone
>
> Urzula Glienecke

Rev. Dr. Urzula Glienecke is a Latvian theologian, artist and activist living in Scotland. A member of the Iona Community and Interfaith Alignment as well as the Edinburgh Interfaith Association. She has lived under occupation. And her prayers come in the form of shape and sound. She has found survival through her connection to the divine that materializes through her hands as they sculpt and through her voice as she sings. Gentle and strong. And grounded.

Our prayers are the work of our hands.

The Sound of Creation

Serge El Helou, from Beirut, Lebanon, sets the oud on his lap and starts a Zoom. People click a button and are transported from around the world into this sacred gathering of prayer. Staying up late in Belgium and the Netherlands, waking up early in Tasmania, from the Pacific Northwest to the deserts of Texas, across the plains, to cities in the northeast of the United States, connected by fiber optics and a desire to hold space together. Serge shares his many years of experience in music therapy, orchestration, teaching music and leading prayer as he sings in Lebanese Arabic, Greek, Syriac, chants from the Lebanese Maronite tradition.

> O Lord, use me for your peace:
> Where there is hatred, let me bring your love;
> To forgive where there is no pardon
> To bring harmony where there is discord
> To bring the truth to the lost
> To share my faith with those who have doubt
> To bring hope to the desperate
> To bring light where there is darkness
> To bring joy where there is sadness

> يَا رب إستَعمِلني لسلامِك
> فأضَعَ الحُبَّ حيثُ البغض
> والمَغفِرَةَ حيثُ الإساءة
> والإتفاقَ حيثُ الخِلاف
> والحقيقَةَ حيثُ الضلال
> والإيمانَ حيثُ الشك
> والرجاءَ حيثُ اليأس
> والنورَ حيثُ الظلمة
> والفَرحَ حيثُ الكآبة
> يَا رب إستَعمِلني لِسلامِك

> Ya Rab, Ista'milni li salamika
> Fa ada' l houbba haythou l-boghd
> Wal maghfirata haythou l-issa-a
> Wal ittifaka haythou l-khilaf
> Wal haqiqata haythou ddalal
> Wal Imana haythou shek
> Wal raja haythou l-ya's

Wan-noura haythou zolma
Wal faraha haythou l ka-aba
Ya Rab, Ista'milni li salamika

The Zoom chat fills with the mention of those who have been displaced by war, genocide, raging fires, blasting storms, poverty, disease, and theft of bodies. Participants are Christian, Orthodox, Protestant and Catholic, Muslim, Jewish, Baha'i and pagan. Serge does not allow the music to pause as he slips deftly from the oud to the piano. Each note resonating, lingering long after it is sounded. And his final chant brings tears.

Qiry'elaison.
Lord, have mercy.
Repeated.
Repeated.
Repeated.

Often through this book I have shared that prayers are so much more than words. They are ordinary actions and sounds and shapes and connections. But sometimes they *are* words. This one elided word in Syriac, sung over and over, reached a place that wove together time zones and traditions and tragedies in a collective cry that allowed each person present to feel spirit in pulses of light transmitting data through thin strands of glass.

From Serge's heart through his instruments of voice and wood and ivory through pulses of light, he encircled each pray-er in the sound of creation.

The invitation to join in the act of creativity comes from Molly Grace Hicks when she leads these same sessions online. Molly, a music therapist, singer/songwriter and Quaker spiritual leader, finds prayer through creative expression using the instrument of her voice, her guitar, writing poetry and crafting collage. She shares her own songs as well as the experiences of her life that brought them into being. As one participant noted, she shares her story in a way that invites us to see ourselves in it and through it. On the morning that the world awoke to the reality of a second unthinkable term of presidency for the United

States, Molly gathered her words to share in poetry with her loved ones.

There's so much I do not know
Yet I know my heart is beating
I can't begin to understand
Yet I understand I'm breathing
There's so much I don't accept
Yet I accept that I'm in shock
I can't find the words to speak
Yet I won't let my voice be blocked

We're not here to be afraid
We're not here to go on hating
We are here to join together
We are here to keep creating

Only loving, only grieving, only healing
Only loving, only grieving, only healing

Molly Grace Hicks

She recognizes that healing lies in continuing to create – and in welcoming others into the lyrics and melodies as a shared prayer. Her closing prayer always extends this invitation in the most beautiful way. She prompts the group with gentle questions: *What brings us joy? For what do we hold gratitude? Where does light show itself in our lives?* Online, the chat overflows with heartfelt responses. In person, Molly carefully records each offering in her little notebook. Then, like folding cream into batter, she blends every contribution into the song she has begun, incorporating the collective ingredients into a melody born of community and connection.

Creating Movement

His fingers flew up and down the keys, pounded chords, curved and curled in the same shape as his spine, head lowered in a deep posture of reverence. For the life of George Floyd, a piece composed around the notes G and F, created and played by Carl Bradley, jazz musician and

Quaker educator. Carl offered the gift he has been given in life – for this life taken. At first I was drawn into the space by my awe of how Carl creates music that has the power to hold and carry so much. By my admiration and fascination and engagement in the performance. But then it was no longer a performance. It became a prayer. The ending movement came. *Homecoming*, Carl named it. He imagined angels, souls welcoming George Floyd home. He said that when playing this he felt as if he was in conversation with George. Those of us sharing the space lowered our heads in respect for the pain that was pouring over the keys. And then we stood. The piece was not finished, but the emotion was so deep and the energy in the room so intense that rising was the only response our bodies could give to match the depth of Carl's expression. Each note carried the weight of grief, the echoes of injustice, and the hope for healing.

Applause would have been inappropriate in response to such an offering. Tears flowed. He had enabled us to mourn collectively. One by one we approached the piano and Carl to say our Amens, to give our thanks, and we found the white ivories red with the blood of his fingers. He had given his life's blood in the playing of this piece. Blood for blood. A sacred offering for a sacred life taken. Prayer as a creative act of remembrance.

Painting the Cave

After my father died, the manse had to be cleaned out because it did not belong to us. It could no longer house the family of the minister who was no longer in the pulpit. At twenty years old, I was not ready to leave my nest. I struggled hard with the loss of a parent and with the loss of the spaces where I felt safe. Where the walls were steeped with the rituals of sabbath prayers and practices. One Saturday when no bread was rising in the kitchen, no soup on the stove, I took myself up to the third floor painting room. I squirted oil paints on the dry palette and scraped them with the knife till they made shades of Grieving Grey, my new concoction. And I began to paint. What came out on the unused canvas that was meant to hold a scene of Hebridean hills was Plato's Cave.

I was a Greek major in college at the time, mainly for the love of learning language, but Plato's *Republic* had captured me. The Allegory of the Cave. The thought that I was a chained prisoner seeing only shadows from real life cast by the sun against the wall of the cave. That beyond what I was seeing in the moment, there was a brightness sitting at my back that was true and real and ideal.

We had visitors in our house. A minister friend of my father's from Edinburgh. Flown from Scotland to help a grieving congregation cope. And I heard him talking to my mother about my painting. It was a good thing, he said. I was expressing my grief creatively. He saw grey upon grey in a blob of oily mess. I balked at being misunderstood. They couldn't see it. The sun that was illuminating the shadows, that gave life to the shadows. The painting allowed me to see that although grief was swallowing up my life, it was the shade of a love so bright and a belief so deep that my father was in that light. It was there. He was there. My philosophical interpretation would not hold weight in my Greek seminar nor would it eventually be considered part of an acceptable exploration in seminary, and why I will not label myself as classicist or theologian. But I had found prayer in the paint, and a shadow of hope in the cave, hope that light sat behind me, even when I could not see it directly.

Practice

LOVING WORDS

It all starts with an idea, ἰδέα.

Patty Krawec in her book, *Becoming Kin*, compares the Christian interpretation of the creation story with the Anishinaabe creation. It all begins with an idea.

In the beginning was the word. An idea. From Gichi-manidoo. From Elohim.

The idea became breath. And breath became water, and land, and sky, and all the creatures, one by one. And then humanity. The Anishinaabe understanding is that humanity is 'the least and neediest of all creation'.[64] Humanity was reliant on all the other forms of creation to exist and they all promised to live in kinship, that all might help one another to survive. No dominion. No stewardship. Kinship.

Plato starts with an idea as well, with an understanding that everything that has being has some ἰδέα, some ideal form of it that exists in the realm of knowing. Is it in opposition to theologies of creation? Let's take that word *idea* back to its origins in the root ἰδε-, from the verb ἰδεῖν (*idein* – *vidēre* – to see). Something that is known because it is seen. To Plato, seen or perceived by the mind, not by the senses, but seen, known. Patty Krawec wonders what it would have been like if the European colonists had come to Turtle Island and had seen and known God in the creation they found there. If they had sought kinship instead of dominion. If it all starts with an idea, let us all start by seeing and knowing that which is the essence of all beings, that we are all creators.

RETHINK ...

our relationship with our gifts of creativity as acts of prayer.

REFRAME ...

the sounds and shapes and colors that reflect our connection to one another and the divine act of creation as embodied prayer.

REIMAGINE ...

picking up a paintbrush although you do not know how to paint, strumming an instrument that you do not know how to play, molding clay into a form, putting words on paper, allowing yourself to create without any expectation other than being present to the act of creation.

Part Six

Practice Peace

Chapter 18
Peace Through Connection

Practice
peace through connection

What Is the Point of Prayer?

During times of immense loss in the world, times of conflict and violence, when grief abounds and anxiety soars, when loss from disaster floods our newsfeed, turning to prayer is a natural response for many. When we are at our own lowest points, when hope is elusive and despair sits as a pit in our core, we are told to pray or that others are praying for us. Sometimes it feels as if it is the only thing we can do, as lives are shattered around us. But these are the times when it is so easy for us to feel as if prayer fails, unless we do the important framing of what our expectations of prayer are.

Prayer for many is certainly a form of asking for what we need, for ourselves and on behalf of others. It is petition and intercession. It can come with urgency and despair, with regret and shame, with hope and longing. We see a world of people we do not know, suffering, and we feel helpless, except in this action of prayer. We carry burdens we cannot voice aloud but know that in prayer we can say the unthinkable. It is a place of vulnerability and brokenness. With the hope that what we offer will be held by someone, something, greater than us, because we cannot hold it alone.

At the very core of interfaith engagement is this intention. In community with those beyond the scope of our experience lies the possibility of being heard and understood and supported and loved. We do not pray for others because we think their prayers won't work. We pray for others because we long for their wellbeing. So to pray for and with someone of a different tradition does just this – it expands the power of connection.

There are some Christians who believe prayers are only legitimate if they are offered in the name of Jesus. To them I would say then offer them in the name of Jesus. It is recorded that when Jesus prayed, he prayed to and in the name of the one that marked the closest relationship of familial bond to him, Abba, Father. The intimacy of the communication is key. If we cultivate this intimacy in partnership, across traditions, every communication with someone from another tradition, every sharing of a fear, a loss, a hope becomes a prayer.

When conflict involves people of different traditions, when one fears their tradition and people feel threatened, can we pray for those of another faith? Can a Muslim pray with and for a Jew? Can Jewish prayers be offered for Muslim and Christian neighbors? Can prayers transcend our differences and reach the level of a united humanity? I believe that not only can we pray together, but perhaps it is a most basic need and the soil in which the seeds of peace are planted.

Before deciding whether we can pray with someone of a different tradition, perhaps we need to clarify what it is we are seeking by praying in the first place. Many traditions address prayer to a divine being.

> Loving God,
> *Barukh ata Adonai Eloheinu, melekh ha'olam*: Blessed are you, Lord our God, King of the Universe,
> *Bismillah Al-Rahman Al-Raheem*: In the name of God, the most Merciful, the Beneficent,
> Merciful Creator, Spirit, One Source.

The act of prayer is at its heart a communication between the pray-er and one, whatever our understanding of it, that will hold us with mercy, grace and love. We turn to prayer needing that communication, to be heard and known, to be assured, to pause in the presence of connection. Sharing a time of prayer with a person of a different tradition does not deny your belief or theirs. It does not dismiss one name of the divine for another. It upholds the foundational purpose of prayer: connection and communication.

Cultivating Connection

Interfaith work has never been about wanting to wash over the differences, blending all into one voice. It has been about embracing all the voices. Many find that in sharing their traditions with others as well as in opening to other traditions, they find themselves strengthened in their own faith. Being engaged in interfaith connections is not a call to abandon one's own tradition. It is a call to stand with those who are also seeking peace. To seek a connection to the divine. To seek something so deep within ourselves and so far beyond ourselves that naming it feels limiting. We cry out to G-d, to Allah, to spirit, HaShem, creator. We call to a God that is not limited, but cosmic, as John Philip Newell says in *Sacred Earth, Sacred Soul*.[65]

Imam Jamal Rahman, Muslim Sufi leader of the Interfaith Community Sanctuary in Seattle, hears the call of compassion and the Qur'an's injunction to connect with one another, each as a distinct individual, as part of the Oneness of God.

From this place of inner spaciousness we begin to understand the wisdom of the much-quoted Qur'anic revelations that God created us in all our diversity of languages, color, gender, and religions so that we might come to know each other (Qur'an 5:48, 49:13).[66]

And Imam Jamal centers his work in this, coming to know others. He gathers with people around the world, sharing stories of Rumi and verses of sacred Islamic texts, sharing the sacred laughter of the Sufis,[67] naming those who are present online as held in rectangles of love, a Zoom-modified version of Rumi's circles of love.

Imam Jamal explains that coming to love one another is a deep reflection of first loving ourselves – finding compassion for ourselves in our most intimate practices of prayer. He invites us into the practice of sacred naming, addressing ourselves with a name of love as would the divine. When he quotes scripture, he quotes it as if it is spoken to him and for him. The ancient sages speak to him directly, Brother Jamal. He urges us to address ourselves not only with the words of this sacred name but also in a tone that communicates self-compassion. It is only through the love we experience for ourselves and through our own traditions that we can reach out with compassion to our neighbor and uphold them in the same radiant love.

Peace, he knows, requires this inner work as well as outer action.

Prayers for World Peace

In 1974, in a world all too familiar with terrorist attacks and bombings, George MacLeod, the founder of the Iona Community, joined with other faith leaders to sign *A Call to Prayer for World Peace*.[68] 'Believing that God is calling us to pray with new purpose and deeper understanding for peace and justice among all people, we invite our fellow believers of all faiths to join in a Week of Prayer for World Peace.

Where people are praying for peace the cause of peace is strengthened by their very act of prayer, for they are themselves becoming immersed in the spirit of peace.

George MacLeod

After fifty years, the call remains the same – the voices of prayer calling out to God by different names, the sacred forms of prayer preserved in ancient words, lifted in song, and embodied in movement. Faith leaders from diverse traditions continue to offer these prayers for peace, now reaching across the world through digital connection. The Week of Prayer for World Peace, coordinated by the office based in England, in collaboration with the Iona Community in Scotland and Interfaith Alignment in the United States, continues to bring together voices from different religious and spiritual traditions. This digital experience is shared by individuals and faith communities worldwide, fostering a collective spirit of peace.

The intention of this collaboration is to encourage those seeking peace for all of humanity to expand their own practices of prayer by embracing the prayers of other traditions, to nurture understanding, empathy and harmony among diverse faith communities, and to raise awareness of the practices and teachings of different traditions. The hope is that through this shared prayer experience, we demonstrate that a true commitment to world peace must include the voices, traditions and hopes of all peoples.

Are prayers enough? No. Never. But they are foundational. They root any action we take, any support we offer, and any pain we endure in something that transcends our circumstances and capabilities.

Prayers remind us that we are more than isolated individuals – they affirm that we are held in divine love and called to be witnesses of that love in the lives of others. And so, it is deeply my belief that our prayers must be shared across traditions.

Kaitlin Curtice reminds us that we are on a journey of being human alongside others of different traditions.[69] She defines the work of sharing our practices as the responsibility we all hold to and for our own tradition, and to and for one another. Prayer is a witness that we are more than our own circumstances and our own capabilities. Learning to pray with someone in their tradition honors them and their struggles and communicates the intention of peace.

May we embrace this journey of being human alongside our siblings who pray in ways that are different from the way we pray. May we be open enough to incorporate new prayers into our own. May we center our life's action in that which honors humanity by valuing the way in which others pray. May we be strong enough to put prayers for peace at the beginning of our work for peace.

With connection and presence and love for ourselves and one another as the core intention of prayer, surely peace will prevail.

Epilogue

Many people have been a part of my journey of coming to understand prayer in my life, as I recognized the life of prayer that enveloped me as a child and met wonderful new friends of many traditions who have shared their practices with me. But without my search for that marble quarry, I may not have fully realized the need to embrace all the ways in which I was lost in order to understand prayer as connection and presence. I kept going because I had to keep going, and that has made all the difference.

Living on Iona for three months and working on this book, I found myself asking many people that I met, 'Have you been to the marble quarry?' Sometimes it just came up in conversation without my initiating it, and sometimes I was curious. Was I the only one who had this trouble finding my way? The rich diversity of responses made it seem as though each person had received a personal prompt to create a story. Everyone knew of the destination. Everyone held wonder for the distinctive marble harvested there. Those who had never been still knew well the white stone married with serpentine that grounds the abbey in the sacredness of the earth on which it stands. It became my touchstone to query those on the island about their relationship to being lost. It became my metaphor for hearing about the prayer life of those around me.

A couple volunteering on the island had just shared a lovely walk there, and a quick picnic, before their evening duties at the abbey. Another, sensing my bewilderment that it was so easy for others, jumped in. 'I don't know where it is, but I'd love to try to find it with you.' A young woman, searching for her own path as a spiritual leader in a tradition that does not yet fully accept the leadership she has to offer, said, 'I want to be with you when you find it.' I came across another couple who live on the island, on a beach below and around the corner from where the quarry sits. I asked them. 'There are quite a few ways to get there,' they said. 'This way is boggy; you'll have to wear your boots. Or veer off to the right when you're coming back from Columba's Bay. We're happy to go with you whichever way you want.'

So many people to walk with me. But I realized I didn't really want to find it. I was enjoying too much the conversation about not finding it. I was loving my analogy of being lost.

One day, a most welcome announcement came. A treat for the abbey volunteers. We were going to stop our jobs early on Friday and take a sail around the island. After three and a half weeks of non-stop rain, the sun was now out in full force. If only I could paint into words the colors of the Sound of Mull waters. So many shades of blues and greens melting into entirely different shades of blue sky. It was glorious. I stepped up on the top deck of the boat and reveled in the company of new friends, ample hugs, and a view of the island from outwards in. Then a tap on my shoulder. There's the marble quarry. We sailed right past it in a matter of seconds. I was looking for magic and sparkles and fulfilment. It looked like nothing. I could barely make out an old piece of machinery from the mining days tucked among the rocks. Just another inlet. No, it had not been about the destination.

The weeks passed, and I continued to delight in the ebb and flow of volunteers and pilgrims to the island, staying later into the fall than I ever had. The nights were drawing in. This book was taking shape. And there were only a few days left to eat my last scones for the year. It was then that my hot-cocoa-loving friend said, 'Do you want to go to the quarry before we leave?' Having arrived on the island after the boat trip of discovery, one of the few who had not been subjected to my quarry queries, she had no idea what her invitation held for me in our final hours on Iona. Yes, yes, let's go to the quarry. I was to meet her at the jetty for the noon ferry. It took me a minute to realize she was not suggesting we go to the marble quarry on Iona but to the granite quarry on Mull, facing us. She arrived with another of our friends, a hot cocoa for each of us for this special trek. We walked ten miles that day, sharing stories and snacks, avoiding a rutting ram, my two Latina friends lapsing into Spanish every now and then, scrambling up rocks, slipping down muddy paths, holding on tightly as we neared the edge and the wind blew us sideways, and there it was. The quarry. *Toremore. Big hill,* basically.

It was not the quarry I had tried to find.

It was a different stone. A different island. A different perspective.

And it was perfect.

As far as we could see to the south there was a tiny break in the cloud cover and rays of sun spilled out on the sea in one solid column, miles from us. Rain was everywhere else, as we huddled, sharing two pairs of waterproofs among the three of us. We sat in silent awe as that spotlight of sun made its way across the sound, lighting up patches of land and sea, until it passed right over us. For seconds we were engulfed in the most vibrant warmth and light, before it carried on to the north and away, leaving a full rainbow that itself materialized and evaporated before a second breath.

We were in the presence of the divine. And one another. And the beauty of our Earth. And I hold this prayer in my heart. That you may stand in the wonder of the rainbow.

Notes

1. The Amidah or Standing Prayer is central to the Jewish daily liturgy. Dhuhr is the second of the five daily Islamic prayers, at the noon hour. And the Lord's Prayer is the prayer that Jesus prayed familiarly to his father. All of these include elements of praise, petition and repentance, and for many following these Abrahamic traditions they are part of a daily routine of prayer.
2. Thomas Merton, *Contemplative Prayer*.
3. Thich Nhat Hanh (1975), *The Miracle of Mindfulness: An Introduction to the Practice of Meditation*.
4. H. Barr (2023), *Collisions of Earth and Sky: Connecting with Nature for Nourishment, Reflection, and Transformation*. Broadleaf Books.
5. Paula D'Arcy as quoted by R. Rohr (2011), *Breathing Under Water: Spirituality and the Twelve Steps*. St. Anthony Messenger Press.
6. https://prayerwrap.skylight.org/
7. H. J. M Nouwen, D. P. McNeill & D. A. Morrison (1982), *Compassion: A Reflection on the Christian Life*. (New York: Image)
8. Naomi Ojumah, Marios Loukas, *The Intriguing History of the Term Sacrum*, Department of Anatomical Sciences, St. George's University, St. George's, Grenada, 2018. https://static1.squarespace.com/static/554037b3e4b0da169013a32f/t/5c06f2141ae6cf9eac24de4b/1543959060660/historyofsacrum_%281%29+%281%29.pdf
9. Cassidy Hall (2023), *Queering Contemplation: Finding Belonging in a Fractured World*. Broadleaf Books.
10. From the Vision Statement of Alignment: Interfaith Contemplative Practices, www.interfaithalignment.org/about
11. https://www.aic-iac.org/wp-content/uploads/Madhvi-SUBRAHMANIAN_Lecture_2oct2018.pdf
12. https://studiopotter.org/serve-divine
13. Eckhart Tolle (2005), *A New Earth: Awakening Your Life's Purpose*. Penguin Group.
14. Lao Tzu (1972), *Tao Te Ching* (G. Feng & J. English, Trans.). Vintage Books. (Original work published ca. 6th century BCE)
15. Bronwen Mayer Henry (2022), *Radioactive Painting: How a Cancer Treatment Lit Up My Creative Practice*.

16 https://www.instagram.com/choosejoyoverperfection/
17 Tricia Hersey (2022), *Rest is Resistance: A Manifesto*. Little, Brown Spark
18 Heidi Barr (2023), *Collisions of Earth and Sky: Connecting with Nature for Nourishment, Reflection, and Transformation*. Broadleaf Books.
19 Heidi Barr (2021), *Slouching Toward Radiance*. Homebound Publications.
20 Chelan Harkin (2024), *The Prophetess: The Return of The Prophet from the Voice of The Divine Feminine*. Hay House Inc.
21 Randly Woodley (2022), *Becoming Rooted: One Hundred Days of Reconnecting with Sacred Earth*. Fortress Press.
22 Barbara Holmes (2021), *Crisis Contemplation: Healing the Wounded Village*. CAC Publishing.
23 ibid.
24 Barack Obama (2006), *The Audacity of Hope: Thoughts on Reclaiming the American Dream*. Crown Publishing Group.
25 https://iona.org.uk/about/our-vision-and-values/
26 Haleh Liza Gafori (2022), *Gold*. NYRB Classics.
27 Plum Village website
28 John Philip Newell (2022), *Sacred Earth, Sacred Soul: A Celebration of Nature and the Sacred in the Celtic Tradition*. HarperCollins B and Blackstone Publishing.
29 Thich Nhat Hanh (1987), *Being Peace*. Parallax Press.
30 Christine Valters Paintner (2021), *Breath Prayer: An Ancient Practice for the Everyday Sacred*. Broadleaf Books.
31 Pema Chödrön (2019), *Welcoming the Unwelcome: Wholehearted Living in a Brokenhearted World*. Shambhala Publications.
32 *Beatha* = life in Scots Gaelic. An English speaker might expect *beatha* to be the word for breath in the phrase *anáil na beatha*, and *anáil* to refer to life, the deep blue of the sky. But perhaps this is another reminder to look more closely at the unexpected beauty held in indigenous language.
33 A. Carmichael (1900), *Carmina Gadelica: Hymns and Incantations* (Vol. 1). Edinburgh: T. and A. Constable.
34 Isaiah 6:8
35 Isaiah 58.9
36 Richard Rohr (2017, February 11), *Daily Meditations*. Center for Action and Contemplation.

37 Virgil's *Aeneid* (IV.173-197)
38 https://www.hinduwebsite.com/gita/wisdom/gita-day14.asp
39 Kaitlin Curtice (2020), *Native: Identity, Belonging, and Rediscovering God*. Brazos Press.
40 ibid
41 John Philip Newell (2021), *Sacred Earth, Sacred Soul*
42 V. Kaur (2020), *See No Stranger: A Memoir and Manifesto of Revolutionary Love*. One World.
43 Naomi Levy, *Einstein and the Rabbi: Searching for the Soul* (p.9). Flatiron Books.
44 Written by Rabbi Menachem Creditor in response to the terrorist attacks of 9/11.
45 Chelan Harkin (2024), *The Prophetess: The Return of The Prophet from the Voice of The Divine Feminine*. Hay House Inc.
46 Tamara Embrey, 'Taming the Wandering Mind: Where Buddhism & Polyvagal Theory Meet' (2022). *Mindfulness Studies Theses*. 69. https://digitalcommons.lesley.edu/mindfulness_theses/69
47 Genesis 21:14-16a, translation by M. Somerville
48 Julian of Norwich, *Revelations of Divine Love*
49 Cornelia B. Horn, 'Between text and sermon: Genesis 21:8-21', 310.
50 Gen 21:17 (trans. M. Somerville)
51 Belden C. Lane (2019), *The Great Conversation: Nature and the Care of the Soul*. Oxford University Press.
52 https://www.starstuffs.com/prayers/fourdirections.html
53 Belden C. Lane (2014), *Backpacking with the Saints: Wilderness Hiking as Spiritual Practice*. Oxford University Press.
54 Belden C. Lane (2019), *The Great Conversation: Nature and the Care of the Soul*. Oxford University Press.
55 Belden C. Lane (2014). Oxford University Press.
56 Patty Krawec (2022). *Becoming Kin: An Indigenous Call to Unforgetting the Past and Reimagining Our Future*. Broadleaf Books.
57 Henri J. M. Nouwen (1996). *Can You Drink the Cup?* Ave Maria Press.
58 J. R. Mahoney Jr., K. T. Denny & R. Mayeux (2014). 'The role of tau in the pathophysiology of Alzheimer's disease'. *International Journal of Alzheimer's Disease*, 2014, Article 3984246.

59 Toba Spitzer (2022), *God Is Here: Reimagining the Divine*. St. Martin's Press.
60 Analysis of the concept of compassion in Rumi's mystical teachings. Javidan Kherad. Retrieved from https://www.javidankherad.ir/article_85277_d7e898342e812fea111 8aa7953dbe4dd.pdf?lang=en
61 Rumi (2004), *The Essential Rumi* (C. Barks, Trans., 2nd ed.). HarperOne.
62 B. D. McLaren (2010), *A New Kind of Christianity: Ten Questions that are Transforming the Faith*. HarperOne.
63 Belden C. Lane (2019), *The Great Conversation: Nature and the Care of the Soul*. Oxford University Press.
64 Patty Krawec (2022). *Becoming Kin: An Indigenous Call to Unforgetting the Past and Reimagining Our Future*. Broadleaf Books.
65 John Philip Newell (2021), *Sacred Earth, Sacred Soul: Celtic Wisdom for Reawakening to What Our Souls Know and Healing the World*. HarperOne.
66 Jamal Rahman, D. Mackenzie, & T. Falcon (2016), *Finding Peace Through Spiritual Practice: The Interfaith Amigos' Guide to Personal, Social, and Environmental Healing*. Skylight Paths Publishing.
67 Jamal Rahman (2014). *Sacred Laughter of the Sufis: Awakening the Soul with the Wisdom of Islam*. SkyLight Paths Publishing.
68 https://weekofprayerforworldpeace.co.uk/
69 Kaitlin Curtice (2020), *Native: Identity, Belonging, and Rediscovering God*. Brazos Press.

About the cover artist

Sondra Rosenberg is an artist and art therapist based in Philadelphia. Working in a range of media and subject matter, she creates art for personal expression, private commissions, and in support of organizations that promote social justice and community development. For the past two decades, Sondra worked as an art therapist, guiding women through a process of accessing and finding visual language for their inner worlds. Her own art practice has been deeply influenced by that approach to creating images. She is interested in the fixed visual expression of shifting mental and emotional states and the ways in which interiors are revealed through surfaces.

Website: www.sondrarosenberg.com
Instagram: @sondraro

Acknowledgements

I thought it was amusing that many of my identities in life started with the letter M. I was given the name of my maternal grandmother, my granny, Margaret. I became a missus for a while, magistra, and minister. But the ones that mean more than anything are Mom and (Aunt) Meg.

To my children and nephew who have taught me about resilience and growth, I marvel every day at the beautiful ways in which you walk this life.

To Susy who has journeyed with me through the lowest lows, to every highpoint and celebration, and all the steps in between. I think I have single-handedly qualified her for an honorary counseling license.

To Peter for marking every turning point in my life. From graduations to baptisms, marriage to divorce, death after death, holding a family and a congregation together when my father died, he was, quite appropriately the rock. Every picture from the garden was a lifeline.

To Barbara for the poems that have carried me there and back, for the hours of simple sharing and walking and noticing the birds.

To Sandy and Pete for making the vision a reality. For opening their hearts and embracing the possibilities with trust and belief and unswerving support.

To Larry for always being there. For sharing the vision and always working to make it better.

To Dawn for greeting each dawn with a text of positive energy, vibes, and love. For never stopping.

To Kaitlin for providing a supportive and grounding space in which to write in community. This book began and ended in that space.

To Sondra for taking a picture of one of my favorite spots on earth and making it into a work of art for the cover of this book. For being able to identify what is held in that space.

To Nick and Sarah for making the shop the most wonderful place to be.

To Caro for making the abbey a place of welcome for people of all traditions in words carefully chosen and for giving me the opportunity to share in that.

To Nancy for helping me move through it all.

To Molly, Barbara, Harold, Asheq, Urzula, and Shelly for dreaming and working and believing that we can build this world with love.

To those very few who carry this last name with me.

To the dozens and dozens of spiritual leaders who have contributed to the offerings of Alignment with chants and songs and dances and paintings and reflections and meditations, prayers in all dimensions.

To Bobby for knocking me down when I was learning to walk and for reaching for my hand when we both need holding up.

And to Baker, my sweet pup, for a love so pure that it can only be divine.

Wild Goose Publications, the publishing house of the Iona Community established in the Celtic Christian tradition of Saint Columba, produces books, e-books, CDs and digital downloads on:

- holistic spirituality
- social justice
- political, peace and environmental issues
- healing and wellbeing
- innovative approaches to worship
- song in worship, including the work of the Wild Goose Resource Group
- material for meditation and reflection

Visit our website at
www.ionabooks.com
for details of all our products and online sales